Sam King QC is a barrister at 4PB. Her main area of practice is in children's law. She is regularly instructed in both private and public law cases. She represents all parties in complex cases involving allegations of sexual abuse or where there are psycho-sexual factors in issue, non-accidental injury, psychiatric ill-health, intractable contact cases and where shared residence is in issue.

Frankie Shama is a barrister at 4PB. He practices in all aspects of children's law, with a focus on private law proceedings and proceedings involving the international movement of children. He accepts instructions at all stages of proceedings, and has a particular interest in intractable contact cases and cases involving allegations of domestic abuse.

A Practical Guide to Parental Alienation in Private and Public Law Children Cases

A Practical Guide to Parental Alienation in Private and Public Law Children Cases

Sam King QC

Frankie Shama

Law Brief Publishing

Published 2022 by Law Brief Publishing, an imprint of Law Brief Publishing Ltd
30 The Parks
Minehead
Somerset
TA24 8BT

www.lawbriefpublishing.com

Paperback: 978-1-913715-18-2

PREFACE

The existence and definition of parental alienation has been the subject to consistent debate over the years. It is now broadly summarised as a child's resistance or hostility towards one parent, which is unjustified and the result of psychological manipulation by the other parent, and is a concept that private children practitioners over recent years have been grappling with increasingly frequently in practice.

This book provides the reader with a history of the emergency of parental alienation as a concept. It charters some of the debate around its definition and scale within the Family Court. It considers the court's general approach to making child arrangements orders in cases where a child rejects or resists spending time with one parent post-separation.

This book also looks at parental alienation in conjunction with allegations of domestic abuse and coercive and controlling behaviour, and the court's application of Practice Direction 12J of the Family Procedure Rules 2010. In considering the intersection between these two issues, it provides an insight into some of the challenges the Family Court faces in assessing a child's rejection of resistance to spending time with the other parent in circumstances where it is unclear if there is a legitimate reason or cause.

Crucially, this provides a unique toolkit for practitioners based on judicial commentary from recent judgments as to how to practically manage cases featuring allegations of parental alienation. It looks at the options available to the court to promote contact and manage a relationship between an alienated child and parent, including but not limited to enforcement options; therapeutic options; section 37 reports and public law interventions; the joinder and separate representation of children, and transfers of residence.

The law in this book is accurate as at 20th June 2022.

Sam King QC
Frankie Shama
June 2022

LIST OF ABBREVIATIONS

Cafcass: Children and Family Court Advisory and Support Service (England)

Cafcass Cymru: Children and Family Court Advisory and Support Service (Wales)

CFA 2014: Children and Families Act 2014

CIAF: Child Impact Assessment Framework

ECHR: European Convention on Human Rights 1950

FCA: Cafcass Family Court Adviser

FPR 2010: Family Procedure Rules 2010

ICFA: Improving Child and Family Arrangements

LASPO 2012: Legal Aid since the Legal Aid, Sentencing and Punishment of Offenders Act 2012

NPS: National Probation Service

NYAS: National Youth Advocacy Service

PAS: Parental Alienation Syndrome

PD: Practice Direction

PFD: President of the Family Division

r16.4 guardian: children's guardian appointed under Rule 16.4 FPR 2010

SPIPs: Separated Parents Information Programmes

The 1989 Act: Children Act 1989

UNCRC: United Nations Convention on the Rights of the Child 1989

WHO: World Health Organisation

CONTENTS

CHAPTER ONE

DEFINING PARENTAL ALIENATION

Introduction

Any consideration of parental alienation must start with the concept of parental responsibility as defined by section 3(1) of the Children Act 1989 ('the 1989 Act'). Parental responsibility includes *"all the rights, duties, powers, responsibilities and authority which by law a parent of a child has in relation to the child and his property."*

The duties and responsibilities that parental responsibility gives rise to has been emphasised throughout the case law. Sir James Munby, when President of the Family Division, observed in *Re H-B (Contact)*[1]:

> *"...parental responsibility is more, much more than a mere lawyer's concept or a principle of law. It is a fundamentally important reflection of the realities of the human condition, of the very essence of the relationship of parent and child. Parental responsibility exists outside and anterior to the law. Parental responsibility involves duties owed by the parent not just to the court. First and foremost, and even more importantly, parental responsibility involves duties owed by each parent to the child."*[2]

Crucially, parental responsibility involves establishing contact between a parent and child when it is safe and beneficial to do so. As stated by McFarlane LJ (as he then was) in the earlier case of *Re W (Direct Contact)*,[3] *"[w]here ... it is plainly in the best interests of a child to spend time with the other parent, tough or not, part of the responsibility of the*

---

1 [2015] EWCA Civ 389

2 ibid., para. 72

3 [2012] EWCA Civ 999

parent with care must be the duty and responsibility to deliver what the child needs, hard though that may be."[4]

Upon separation, the majority of parents are able to foster a cooperative co-parenting relationship and make arrangements by agreement about the division of the children's time. In the majority of cases, the issue with which the court has to deal is how much time the subject children are to spend with each parent, rather than the principle of contact. Therefore, once the regime is defined, the pattern is established and the issue is resolved. However, there are a number of cases where the contact agreed or ordered does not take place. In such cases, the court may be asked to intervene.

The case law has emphasised that parental responsibility in such circumstances necessitates a parent not unreasonably 'shirking' responsibility. McFarlane LJ in *Re W (Direct Contact)* notes that it is "*not … acceptable for a parent to shirk that responsibility and simply say 'no' to reasonable strategies designed to improve the situation in this regard.*"[5] This has been endorsed by Sir James Munby in *Re H-B (Contact)*, who notes that it is similarly not "*acceptable for a parent to shirk their responsibility by sheltering behind the assertion that the child will not do, or even that the child is adamantly opposed to doing something…*"[6] He goes on to note:

> *"As McFarlane LJ observed (para 75)* [of *Re W (Direct Contact)*], *the responsibility of being a parent can be tough, it may be 'a very big ask'. But that is what parenting is all about. There are many things which they ought to do that children may not want to do or even refuse to do: going to the dentist, going to visit some 'boring' elderly relative, going to school, doing homework or sitting an examination, the list is endless. The parent's job, exercising all their parental skills, techniques and stratagems – which may include use of both the carrot and the stick and, in the case of the older child, reason and argument –, is to get the child to do what it does not want to do. That the child's refusal cannot as such be a justification for parental failure is clear: after all, children*

4 ibid., para. 75

5 ibid., para. 78

6 *Re H-B (Contact)* [2015] EWCA Civ 389, para. 74

whose education or health is prejudiced by parental shortcomings may be taken away from their parents and put into public care."[7]

The key tension that the court will need to grapple with in circumstances where there is a refusal or resistance by a child to contact is *why* that contact is not taking place. On the one hand, it may be argued that contact is not taking place for perfectly legitimate reasons. On the other, it may be argued that contact is being opposed or frustrated by one parent. Allegations may be made that one parent is contributing to the intractable situation, or that they are alienating the child. It is this tension which is the subject of this book.

The differences between implacable hostility, Parental Alienation Syndrome and parental alienation

The last two decades have seen the evolution in our understanding of how and why the relationship between a child and their parent can be compromised or frustrated. While the focus has been on estrangement for reasons of negative parental influence, there are reasons other than the process of hostile manipulation, which must be distinguished. The court has tried to grapple with this issue through use of a variety of terms, including implacable hostility, Parental Alienation Syndrome, and parental alienation.

Implacable hostility

The use of implacable hostility as a term of art in cases of thwarted parent child relationships[8], can be traced back as far back as the 1990s including in the decision of *Re J (A Minor) (Contact),*[9] when Balcombe LJ suggested that:

"... judges should be very reluctant to allow the implacable hostility of one parent (usually the parent who has a residence order in his or her

---

7 ibid., para. 75

8 See *Re W (Direct Contact)* [2012] EWCA Civ 999; *Re J-M (Child)* [2014] EWCA Civ 434; *Re Q (Implacable Contact Dispute)* [2015] EWCA Civ 991; and *Re A (A Child)* [2015] EWCA Civ 910.

9 [1994] 1 FLR 729

favour), to deter them from making a contact order where they believe the child's welfare requires it. The danger of allowing the implacable hostility of the residential parent (usually the mother) to frustrate the court's decision is too obvious to require repetition on my part."[10]

However, the modern understanding of the question of how and why the relationship between a child and their parent can be compromised or frustrated really started with *Re L, Re V, Re M and Re H (Contact: Domestic Violence).*[11] In this decision, the court considered expert psychiatric evidence that had been put before it from Drs Sturge and Glaser[12], which provided the court with a definition in the form of reasons for a resident parent taking a position of implacable hostility. These included:

"(a) A fully justified fear of harm or abduction resulting from any direct contact with the non-resident parent.

(b) A fear of violence or other threat and menace to herself if the non-resident parent has indirect contact to her through the child, i.e. it could lead to direct contact.

(c) Post-traumatic symptoms in the custodial parent which are acutely exacerbated by the prospect or the fact of contact.

(d) The aftermath of a relationship in which there was a marked imbalance in the power exercised by the two parents and where the mother fears she will be wholly undermined and become helpless and totally inadequate again if there is any channel of contact between herself and the ex-partner, even when that only involves the child. The child can be used as a weapon in such a bid to continue to hold power over the mother. As in (a), (b), and (c) above this can be a sequelae of domestic violence.

---

10 ibid., at 736

11 [2000] EWCA Civ 194; [2002] 2 FLR 334

12 Drs Sturges and Glaser, 'Contact and domestic violence: the experts court report', [2000] Fam Law 615

(e) Wholly biased hostility which is not based on real events or experience. This may be conscious and malign or perceived to be true. The latter encompass the full continuum from misperceptions and misunderstandings through overvalued ideas to delusional states. The former may result from a simple wish to wipe the slate clean and start again and can be seen after relationships that were initially highly romantic or idealised and for the breakdown of which the woman can only account for by vilifying the partner in order to avoid facing the possibility that the breakdown in the relationship was her failure and amounts to rejection."

Parental Alienation Syndrome (PAS)

By the time *Re L, Re V, Re M and Re H (Contact: Domestic Violence)* was before the court the term PAS had been coined, and a tension existed between the definition of implacable hostility and how and if it differed from PAS. From 1985 onwards the child psychologist Richard Gardner produced a number of books and articles on the subject of PAS, and provided the following definition:

"The parental alienation syndrome (PAS) is a childhood disorder that arises almost exclusively in the context of child-custody disputes. Its primary manifestation is the child's campaign of denigration against a good, loving parent—a campaign that has no justification. It results from the combination of a programming (brainwashing) parent's indoctrinations and the child's own contributions to the vilification of the target parent. When true parental abuse and/or neglect is present, the child's animosity may be justified and so the parental alienation syndrome explanation for the child's hostility is not applicable."[13]

In *Re L, Re V, Re M and Re H (Contact: Domestic Violence)*, in the part of Dame Butler-Sloss's (then PFD)judgment devoted to *Re M*, while recognising that *"some parents, particularly mothers, are responsible for alienating their children from their father's without good reason"*, it was

[13] Richard A. Gardner, M.D., 'The Parental Alienation Syndrome: Past, Present and Future', based on the address presented to the International Conference of the Parental Alienation Syndrome held in Frankfurt/ Main, Germany, 18-19 October 2002 (http://richardagardner.com/ar22)

noted that the report from Drs Sturges and Glaser observed that the use of PAS was both controversial—its existence was "*not recognised*" and "*not universally accepted*"—and potentially unhelpful in that it pathologised behaviour (and its effect) and suggested a need for mental health professionals to play an expert role.[14] There was a risk arising from this of incorrect assumptions being made about the process at work and, as a corollary, the intervention needed to address it. Following the Court of Appeal's decision and the work of Drs Sturges and Glaser the term PAS fell out of favour, and it was considered to be better to discuss the issue of resistance to parental contact in the context of implacable hostility cases or implacable situations.

Crucially, while PAS assumes a cause (from a misguided or malign resident parent), leading to prescribed intervention, implacable hostility is simply a statement aimed at understanding particular situations, for which a range of explanations are possible, and with no single prescribed solution.

Eighteen years after *Re L, Re V, Re M and Re H (Contact: Domestic Violence)*, in his keynote address to the NAGALRO Annual Conference when McFarlane LJ (as he then was) stated:

> *"It is, in my view, unhelpful to look in every such case to see if it is possible to identify a formal label of "Parental Alienation Syndrome". In such cases, that there has been 'alienation', with a small 'A', will normally be a given; it is that factor which will often render the case 'intractable'. The existence of alienation of itself can only be damaging to a child. It must be grim to grow up having a profoundly negative view of one of your parents. In some cases such a negative view may be justified by the actions of that parent, but often life is not so black and white and a more nuanced, ordinary and tolerable view of both parents will have been justified had an imbalanced status quo as to contact not become established."*[15]

14 *Re L, Re V, Re M and Re H (Contact: Domestic Violence)* [2000] EWCA Civ 194; [2002] 2 FLR 334 at 351

15 Sir Andrew McFarlane, NAGALRO Annual Conference – Keynote Address, 'Contact: A Point of View', 19 March 2018

McFarlane LJ (as he then was) further noted in his keynote address at the Families Need Fathers Conference 2018:

> *"I wish to say something now about "alienation". For some time there has been debate as to whether or not the holy grail of "parental alienation syndrome" actually exists. For my part, I have never regarded it as important to determine definitively whether or not psychologists or psychiatrists would be justified in attributing the label "syndrome" to any particular behaviour in this regard. In time gone by, there was similar debate as to whether a diagnosis could be made of "Munchhausen's Syndrome by Proxy" in such cases the focus of the Family Court, rightly, moved away from any psychological/psychiatric debate in order to concentrate on the particular behaviour of the particular parent in relation to the particular child in each individual case. If that behaviour was found to be abusive then action was taken, irrespective of whether or not a diagnosis of a particular personality or mental health condition in the parent could be made.*
>
> *In my view, "alienation" should be approached in the same way. From my experience as a first instance judge, albeit now more than 7 years ago, I readily accept that in some cases a parent can, either deliberately or inadvertently, turn the mind of their child against the other parent so that the child holds a wholly negative view of that other parent where such a negative view cannot be justified by reason of any past behaviour or any aspect of the parent-child relationship. Further, where that state of affairs has come to pass, it is likely to be emotionally harmful for the child to grow up in circumstances which maintain an unjustified and wholly negative view of the absent parent."*[16]

Also in 2018, in the case of *Re D (A Child: Parental Alienation)*[17], HHJ Bellamy deployed the heading 'Parental Alienation' and made explicit

---

(https://law.bloomsburyprofessional.com/blog/nagalro-conference-2018-keynote-address)

16 Lord Justice McFarlane, 'Families Need Fathers Conference 2018 – Keynote Address by Lord Justice McFarlane', 25 June 2018 (https://www.judiciary.uk/wp-content/uploads/2018/06/speech-lj-mcfarlane-fnf.pdf)

17 [2018] EWFC B64

reference to the fault-lines in the debate surrounding PAS and parental alienation:

> *"Parental alienation syndrome is a theory first propounded by American child psychiatrist Richard Gardner in 1985. For the mother, Mr Hadden MBE has produced an article published by Carol S Bruch in 2001,* Parental alienation syndrome and parental alienation: getting it wrong in child custody cases, *in which the author systematically demolishes Gardner's approach, which she refers to as 'junk science'. For my part I have no difficulty in accepting Bruch's criticisms of Gardner's work in that area. That does not, though, diminish the very real concerns about the problem of alienation in general and parental alienation in particular."*[18]

It remains the case that the term PAS is largely unused nowadays, and the need to formally label it as a 'syndrome' has fallen away. The proponents for and against the recognition of both the terms parental alienation and PAS continue to argue on one side or another, and no doubt Peter Jackson LJ hoped to quieten what some consider to be a distracting discourse in relation to nomenclature, noting in *Re S (Parental Alienation: Cult)*[19]:

> *"As to alienation, we do not intend to add to the issue about labels. We agree with Sir Andrew McFarlane (see [2018] Fam Law 988) that where behaviour is abusive, protective action must be considered whether or not the behaviour arises from a syndrome or diagnosed condition."*[20]

Parental alienation

In discussing parental alienation in the 2011 case of *Re S (Transfer of Residence)*[21], HHJ Bellamy discusses the expert evidence provided by child and adolescent psychiatrist, Dr Weir, saying as follows:

---

[18] ibid., para. 167

[19] [2020] EWCA Civ 568

[20] ibid., para. 8

[21] [2010] EWHC B19 (Fam)

"43. In his first report Dr Weir gave this description of the concept of alienation:

> *'There are children who show an extraordinary degree of animosity towards a parent with whom they once had a loving relationship. Most of these children will show some or all of [a cluster of psychological responses]. Within an individual child (and between children in the same family) the presence of the features can vary rapidly over time and place, but in their full manifestation are so surprising and unique as to be unforgettable. The proposed term "Alienation" applies only to the cluster of psychological responses in the child with no need to presume a deliberate campaign of denigration by one parent. There is now research data supporting a multifactorial aetiology for "Alienation" following parental separation, involving contributions from both parents and vulnerabilities within the child.'*

44. In my judgment of 15 June 2009 I accepted both the concept of alienation and the fact that S is alienated from his father. For some weeks after the local authority became involved in this case it was unclear to me whether the local authority accepted either the concept of alienation or Dr Weir's assessment that S is alienated from his father. I note that in the Court of Appeal, counsel for the local authority described Dr Weir as 'an evangelist for the concept of alienation'. [...]

46. In the light of the considerable body of evidence I have heard and read in this case over the last 3 years, the research literature that has been produced and my experience of dealing with other high conflict cases involving different experts, I am satisfied that Dr Weir's evidence as to the concept of alienation as a feature of some high conflict parental disputes may today be regarded as being mainstream."[22]

The key question is: does parental alienation amount to the same thing as implacable hostility? Many contend that the two do not entirely or comfortably overlap. That is unsurprising given the more expansive definition of implacable hostility offered by Drs Sturges and Glaser in

[22] ibid., paras. 43-44 & 46

the report considered above, sees arguably only four of the five paragraphs characterised as examples of implacable hostility matching the defining features of parental alienation, which as we shall come onto, are largely focused around *unjustified* responses. Only (e) of Drs Sturges' and Glaser's definition refers to hostility which is *not* based on real events or experience.

The use of the term parental alienation (minus the word 'syndrome') has become the preferred term, and whilst initially used interchangeably with intractable hostility in judgments, it appears to have now come to describe a different phenomenon.

In a podcast from Community Care from September 2018[23], Sarah Parsons, principal social worker and assistant director at the Children and Family Court Advisory and Support Service ('Cafcass') said:

> *"I think one of the things that we would want to add to that is that 'implacable hostility' is an adult-centred term. It's about the relationship between the adults. What we want to do all the time as children's social workers is to think of the impact of that behaviour on the child, that the implacable hostilities between two parents doesn't really convey the same sense of meaning as alienation, which intrinsically involves the child aligning with one parent or the other and rejecting one parent. So it's a term used but it is distinctly different from parental alienation."*

Similarly, in the more recent case law, the clearest definition of implacable hostility can be found in *Re B (a child)*[24] where King LJ explains that:

> *"Implacable hostility is exactly that: a case where one parent has become (usually irrationally and for poor motives) implacably opposed to contact taking place between a child and his or her absent parent.*

23 Community Care, 'Parental alienation: what is it and how it's different from implacable hostility', 5 September 2018 (https://www.communitycare.co.uk/2018/09/05/parental-alienation-different-implacable-hostility/)

24 [2016] EWCA Civ 1088

That is . . . or may be very different from a case where a child has become alienated from a parent."[25]

It is therefore possible to differentiate between the two concepts.

In 2019 there was a cluster of cases in which the term parental alienation featured in the title: *Re T (Parental Alienation)*[26] before HHJ Raeside (sitting as a High Court Judge); *Re H (Parental Alienation)*[27] before Keehan J and *Re A (Children) (Parental Alienation)*[28] before HHJ Wildblood QC. Following that, the trend has continued with a series of four cases in 2020 in respect of the same children: *Re A and B (Parental Alienation: No.1, No.2, No.3 and No.4)*.[29] In those four cases, which also came before Keehan J, the court was entirely comfortable with using the label parental alienation, explicitly referring to the expertise of those instructed as experts in the field of parental alienation.[30]

Anecdotally, it is also increasingly common in practice to hear the phrase parental alienation used frequently by lay clients seeking to convey a sense of disaffection with the quality and quantity of time spent with their children.

Even so, whilst parental alienation has become the preferred term, its use may still remain relatively rare in the context of private children law cases. In October 2021, Lucy Reed published an article through the Transparency Project entitled 'Parental Alienation – what can we tell from published judgments?'[31] In preparation for writing the article, she undertook research into the case law and recorded that her survey of the

---

25 ibid., para. 10

26 [2019] EWHC 3854 (Fam)

27 [2019] EWHC 2723 (Fam)

28 [2019] EWFC B56

29 [2020] EHWC 3366; [2021] EWHC 2601 (Fam); [2021] EWHC 2602 (Fam); [2021] EWHC 2603 (Fam)

30 *Re A and B (Parental Alienation: No.3)* [2020] EWHC 3366 (Fam), para. 23

31 Lucy Reed, 'Parental Alienation – what can we tell from published judgments', The Transparency Project, 17 October 2021 (https://www.transparencyproject.org.uk/parental-alienation-what-can-we-tell-from-published-judgments/)

preceding year identified only 29 judgments which specifically included the terms 'parental alienation' and 'alienation.' That said, it was noted that these published judgments are unlikely to be a representative sample – most of the published judgments for example were from judges of High Court level, and the sample does not adequately capture the work of most Circuit Judges, District Judges and Magistrates sitting up and down the country.

Defining parental alienation

There is a significant amount of academic debate in respect of the definition of parental alienation. Whilst largely outside the scope of this book, the 2018 report published by Cascade Children's Social Care Research and Development Centre outlines some of the research literature. The report arrives at a generally accepted position that parental alienation refers to *"the unwarranted rejection of the non-custodial parent characterised by the child's extreme negativity towards the alienated parent due to the deliberate or unintentional actions of the alienating parent so as to adversely affect the relationship with the alienated parent."*[32] It notes however that there is also a paucity of empirical research into parental alienation, and what exists is dominated by a few key authors.

An important step in the defining and recognising parental alienation in the UK came in October 2018, when Cafcass published their assessment framework to support Family Court Advisers ('FCAs') in advising the court in private law children matters. The assessment framework is called the Child Impact Assessment Framework ('CIAF'), and it brought together both new and existing guidance. It explicitly engages with the issue of parental alienation, providing guidance and tools for FCAs to use in managing cases in which a child refused or resisted spending time with one of their parents.

[32] Doughty, J., Maxwell, N., and Slater, T., 'Review of Research and Case Law on Parental Alienation', Cascade Children's Social Care Research and Development Centre commissioned by Cafcass Cymru, April 2018 (https://gov.wales/sites/default/files/publications/2018-05/review-of-research-and-case-law-on-parental-alienation.pdf), page 27, based on A.J.L. Baker and D.C. Darnall, 'A Construct Study of the Eight Symptoms of Severe Parental Alienation Syndrome', Journal of Divorce and Remarriage (2007), 47(1-2), 55-75

The Cafcass website and guidelines now fully embrace and employ the terminology of parental alienation. While recognising that there is no single accepted definition, Cafcass recognises parental alienation as *"the unjustified resistance or hostility from a child towards one parent as a result of the psychological manipulation by the other parent."*[33] Importantly, while wishing to avoid labels, the Cafcass definition is given express endorsement by Peter Jackson LJ in Court of Appeal in *Re S (Parental Alienation: Cult)*. It is noted:

> *"For working purposes, the CAFCASS definition of alienation is sufficient:*
>
> > *"When a child's resistance/hostility towards one parent is not justified and is the result of psychological manipulation by the other parent."*
>
> *To that may be added that the manipulation of the child by the other parent need not be malicious or even deliberate. It is the process that matters, not the motive."*[34]

Indeed, frequently the court is met with situations where the hostile parent tells the court they are supportive of contact but the child is resistant, failing to acknowledge their behaviour may be causative (intentionally or inadvertently) in shaping or influencing the child's views. It is easy, therefore, to see why Peter Jackson LJ added the last paragraph to the Cafcass definition.

Alienating behaviours

The starting point in any cases involving allegations of alienation will be determining what is going on for the child. In *Re E (A Child)*[35], Hedley J puts it as follows:

---

33 Cafcass, 'Cafcass reissues position on parental alienation', 14 January 2021 (https://www.cafcass.gov.uk/2021/01/14/cafcass-reissues-position-on-parental-alienation/)

34 *Re S (Parental Alienation: Cult)* [2020] EWCA Civ 568, para. 8

35 [2011] EWHC 3521 (Fam)

"It is important for me to recognise in cases such as this that one must take seriously the fact that child expresses firm opposition to contact, but one must ask seriously: why that is the case? It may be that the child genuinely opposes contact. In those cases it is usually relatively simple, but not always, but usually relatively simple to identify a reason or reasons why that should be so. In other cases one finds opposition that is, of course, superficially real and genuine but is in fact a protection for the child against finding herself in endless conflict with the residential parent, upon whom, as in this case, she is wholly dependent…"[36]

The CIAF encourages FCAs to look at the child's experience as a whole, and the various reasons *why* a child may resist post-separation time with a parent. This can include appropriate justified rejection situations due to domestic abuse or other forms of harmful parenting such as substance misuse and legitimate affinity, alignment or attachment issues, all of which may provide legitimate explanations as to a child's objections (as will be further explored in **Chapter 3: Parental alienation and domestic abuse**). However, as part of the evaluation of the reasons for a child's resistance, parental alienation should be considered, and whether the child is being subjected to alienating behaviours.

Cafcass defines alienating behaviours as *"behaviours to describe circumstances where there is an ongoing pattern of negative attitudes, beliefs and behaviours of one parent (or carer) that have the potential or expressed intent to undermine or obstruct the child's relationship with the other parent. It is one of a number of reasons why a child may reject or resist spending time with one parent post-separation."*[37]

Cafcass notes that behaviours and indicators can include negative attitudes, and behaviours and beliefs that denigrate, demean, vilify, malign, ridicule or dismiss the child's other parent. It includes conveying false beliefs or stories to, and withholding positive information from the child about the other parent together with the relative absence of

36 ibid., para. 31

37 Cafcass, 'Behaviours – what are alienating behaviours?' (https://www.cafcass.gov.uk/grown-ups/parents-and-carers/divorce-and-separation/what-to-expect-from-cafcass/alienating-behaviours/)

observable positive attitudes and behaviours. It also includes spurning, terrorising, isolating, corrupting or exploiting, and not responding appropriately to the child's emotional needs. These tactics can foster a false belief that the parent who has been subject to the alienating behaviour is dangerous or unworthy. As a result of these experiences, children may adapt their own behaviours and feelings to the alienating parent to ensure that their attachment needs are met.[38]

Cafcass FCAs are encouraged to utilise a number of tools developed as part of the CIAF, including the 'Alienating Behaviours Thinking Tool',[39] in order to assist with identifying alienation behaviours in children. This tool states that behaviours exhibited by a child where they have experienced alienation or implacable hostility include (but are not limited to):

- *The child's opinion of a parent is **unjustifiably** one sided, all good or all bad; idealises one parent and devalues the other.*

- *Trivial, false, weak and/or irrational reasons to justify dislike or hatred.*

- *Allegations of harm are made against the rejected parent which, following investigation are either unsubstantiated or found not to have occurred.*

- *Reactions and perceptions are unjustified or disproportionate to parent's behaviours. This is often based around a single incident or alleged incident.*

- *Talks openly and without prompting about the rejected parent's perceived shortcomings*

- *Revises history to eliminate or diminish the positive memories of the previously beneficial experiences with the rejected parent. May report events that they could not possibly remember.*

---

38 ibid.

39 Available at: https://www.cafcass.gov.uk/grown-ups/professionals/ciaf/resources-for-assessing-child-refusal-resistance/

- *Extends dislike/ hatred to extended family of rejected parent (rejection by association).*

- *Where otherwise compliant children appear to defy the resident parent's verbal and observed attempts to encourage contact.*

- *No guilt, or ambivalence regarding their attitude towards the rejected parent.*

- *Speech about rejected parent appears scripted, it has an artificial quality; no conviction; uses adult language; has a rehearsed quality.*

- *Claims to be fearful but is aggressive, confrontational, even belligerent.*

- *Otherwise compliant children who do not recognise the authority of professionals or the court.*

It also identifies behaviours which may be demonstrated by a parent who intermittently or persistently alienates a child. These include (but again are not limited to):

- *Actively denigrates and exaggerates flaws of the other parent to the child, directly or indirectly e.g. may ask others to do this also.*

- *A resident parent with authority over all aspects of a child's life but abdicates parental responsibility regarding the relationship with the other parent (e.g. 'I won't make them do something they don't want to do.')*

- *A resident parent who will not 'force' or 'drag' a child to contact and uses those or other negatively loaded terms.*

- *Coaches or instructs the child in what to say to professionals and others about negative experiences of the rejected parent.*

- *Where a resident parent applies to the court to reduce the amount of time the child spends with the other parent, particularly where there have been previous proceedings, and there appear to be no safety or welfare issues.*

- *Where a resident parent moves locality without agreement and a shared care arrangement or significant contact arrangement becomes unworkable.*

- *Refusal to hear positive comments about other parent; quick to discount child's good times as trivial and unimportant.*

- *Overt and covert threats to withdraw love and affection from child unless other parent, and/or siblings that live with the other parent, are rejected.*

- *Expresses no concern or empathy that the child is missing out on a previously positive relationship with the other parent. Is disinterested in the impact this may have on their development and identity.*

- *Portrays the other parent as dangerous (**and this is not justified**). False or fabricated allegations of physical abuse, sexual, and/or emotional abuse or a single incident has disproportionate levels of fear or risk associated.*

- *Telephone messages, gifts, and communications from the other parent to child are persistently destroyed, ignored, or passed on to the child with disdain.*

- *False information repeated to child; distorts history and may make false allegations to professionals and in court proceedings.*

- *Does not correct child's rude, defiant behaviour directed toward the other parent but would not permit child to do this with others.*

- *Is reluctant to allow professionals to make arrangements to see the child privately or tries to exert control over the enquiries the professional makes.*

- *Makes the child aware of their own distress and emotional fragility.*

- *Where a resident parent insists on being present (in person or on media) during contact time that has been assessed as safe or where it has been previously agreed was safe, without significant event to alter this view.*

- *Makes complaints against professionals for harming the children by promoting time with the other parent.*

The above lists do not however capture the full spectrum of alienating behaviours and there are a number of case law examples throughout this book which may prove useful. At perhaps the most extreme end is a parent making false allegations of sexual abuse,[40] including inculcating a child with false beliefs of the same.[41]

The tool finally outlines behaviours that may be exhibited by a rejected parent which may contribute to the dynamic, including (but not limited to):

- *Lacks empathetic connection to the child.*

- *Ineffective pursuit of the child. Pushes calls and communications, unannounced appearances at school or activities that the child perceives as embarrassing.*

- *Harsh, rigid, and punitive parenting style (uses authoritarian parenting style as the dominant strategy). This is particularly damaging when relating to older children who are striving for independence.*

- *Treats the child as much younger than their age, possibly due to not having spent time with the child for a significant period of time.*

- *Loses temper, angry, demanding, intimidating character traits, but not to level of abuse.*

- *Outrage at challenge to his/her authority.*

- *Apportions blame to widespread sources including other parent, child, extended family, professionals and the court.*

- *Counter-rejecting behaviour. Passivity or withdrawal in the face of the child's resistance or rejection of them.*[42]

---

40 See for example *Re Y (A Child: Private Law: Fact Finding)* [2014] EWHC 486 (Fam)

41 See for example *Re A (Suspended Residence Order)* [2009] EWHC 1576 (Fam)

42 For a decision in which the court refused to make a finding of parental alienation against the mother, and instead concluded that the father's own inability to accept the child had a voice of his own and lack of insight into the child's needs had caused the child emotional harm, see *Re A (A Child)* [2021] 9 WLUK 485.

Whilst this tool is for use by FCAs in their work with families, the above lists are helpful both in asserting and defending claims of parental alienation: using the list as a notional framework that either captures what is happening in a case, or to show that a case departs from the features identified, can be effective and illuminating.

It is noted that although there is some general agreement in respect of behaviours and strategies employed in parental alienation, it does have multiple 'determinants', including behaviours and characteristics of the alienating parent, alienated parent and the child. In respect of the child, these are often compounded by the child's age and developmental stage, as well as their personality traits, and the extent to which the child internalises negative consequences of triangulation. This has led to several measures and tests for parental alienation, and it is acknowledged that more research is needed on the issue.[43]

The impact of parental alienation

It is widely acknowledged that the harm caused by alienation is immediate, in that it blocks a child's relationship with one parent, and potentially extended family, and all the positive experiences which may flow from this. It may have enduring effects, leading to a child's relationships being compromised into adulthood, and mean the complete loss of a relationship with the alienated parent beyond the child's minority.

However, the harm that can be caused to the child may go beyond this. In the matter of *Re A and B (Parental Alienation: No. 1)*, a decision of Keehan J, the court received expert evidence from Dr Julet Butler (psychiatrist) in respect of the impact of the parental conflict and

---

43 See Doughty, J., Maxwell, N., and Slater, T., 'Review of Research and Case Law on Parental Alienation', Cascade Children's Social Care Research and Development Centre commissioned by Cafcass Cymru, April 2018 (https://gov.wales/sites/default/files/publications/2018-05/review-of-research-and-case-law-on-parental-alienation.pdf), para 4.3 at page 19 onwards for an extensive overview of the research into the determinants of parental alienation, and para. 4.7 at page 27.

mother's intractable position on the two subject children, Child A and Child B, both in the immediate and the long-term.

In respect of Child A, it was noted that she presented with evidence of disordered attachment development and increased risk of mental health problems as a result of being exposed to parental conflict. She presented as pseudo mature, and adult-like in manner due to being placed in situations, and being forced to cope in situations, beyond her emotional age and ability. Dr Butler noted:

> *"In my opinion, Child A is triangulated within the parental conflict. Currently, she has taken up a role whereby she is the one maintaining the conflict with The Father which allows The Mother to stand back and appear to be the reasonable adult who wants to end the conflict. The Mother would state, however, it is impossible for her to do that as the children are refusing to see their dad. Thus, she cannot do anything to effect change. Child A has had to develop a complex attachment strategy in order to survive in this environment. In my opinion, in her relationship with her mother The Mother, she is presenting with a compulsive compliant compulsive* [sic] *caregiving attachment theory. Children who develop this attachment pattern do so in the face of persistently unavailable care. It also develops from children who have to manage unpredictable but repeated danger. Parental conflict post-separation is one of the most dangerous environments children have to survive. They learn that it is best not to present their needs or to distress adults. At best, it may not elicit any response. At worse, it could provoke attack. Children develop the strategy of being pleasing and helpful as a means of understanding."*[44]

It was observed that part of this involved Child A portraying her father in a way which did not match the reality of how he presented. In terms of the long-term implications, Dr Butler noted:

> *"Child A is at risk of developing depression and anxiety as an adolescent and an adult. These experiences risk impacting on her capacity to form safe relationships. She is at high risk of developing abusive relationships as an adult and of struggling as a parent herself. Her parents need to*

[44] *Re A and B (Parental Alienation: No.1)* [2020] EWHC 3366 (Fam)., para. 14

effect significant change soon in order to mitigate against the emotional harm that has already been done to Child A and her capacity to manage in relationships."[45]

In respect of Child B, it was noted that he presented with a depressive disorder, with a risk that he was suicidal. He missed his father but felt hopeless and helpless. It was also noted that Child B showed signs of disordered attachment development – he evinced a compulsive compliant caregiving attachment strategy, rejecting his father because that was what was required by his sister and mother. Perhaps most shockingly is the following summary by Dr Butler of Child B's presentation:

> *"In summary, Child B presents as a child who has an insecure attachment relationship with both his parents. He also sees his sister as a parental figure but she also makes him anxious. Therefore, he has no one to whom he can express any feelings of loss for his dad. He sees no possibility for change in his father which is his sister's position also. He did not think that anything could happen that he could forgive his father but as we spoke about this, he became increasingly dysfluent. By the end, he was just staring at himself in the mirror. I think he had emotionally shut down. I was concerned for his mental health. I was concerned at Child B's mental health having met with him. I think there is evidence of depressive disorder. This was mainly manifested when he talked about school. He broke down completely and tears were rolling down his face. Child B told me, 'Everyone thinks I'm disgusting.' He does not feel he can tell anyone about it. He feels that people are physically moving away from him and they do not want to be close to him. I think there is a risk that he is projecting the loss of his father into school and acting it out there. Sadly, his mother is minimising of this and so he has to deal with the distress himself."*[46]

The harm being caused to these children in the immediate, and the potential for lasting long-term harm in the future, could not have been

---

45 ibid., para. 16

46 ibid., para. 18

made clearer in this case. It serves as a powerful reminder of the implications of ongoing parental conflict and alienation upon children.

The paucity of empirical research into parental alienation however makes establishing both the prevalence and long-term effects of parental alienation difficult.[47]

The World Health Organisation ('WHO')

On 25 May 2019, it appeared that the World Health Organisation (WHO) included 'parental alienation' in the International Classification of Diseases (ICD-11) as a synonym/index term for "*caregiver-child relationship problem*" (QE52.0) which was described as a "*substantial and sustained dissatisfaction within a caregiver-child relationship associated with significant disturbance in functioning.*" The ICD is the diagnostic classification standard for all clinical and research purposes which defines diseases, disorders and other related health conditions. Its purpose is to provide internationally standardised classification for health diagnosis, to count health events and episodes of contact with healthcare for statistical purposes. Whilst not an entirely separate diagnosis, the potential inclusion of parental alienation as an index term for search purposes was an important step in its recognition as a mental health phenomenon, in particular in the wake of the campaign work led by Professor William Bernet, head of the Parental Alienation Study Group.[48]

However, it was something of a controversial step and attracted much criticism from women's rights groups in particular[49] over its potential

---

[47] The issue of the impact of alienation is largely outside the scope of this book, however readers are encouraged to consider Doughty, J., Maxwell, N., and Slater, T., 'Review of Research and Case Law on Parental Alienation', Cascade Children's Social Care Research and Development Centre commissioned by Cafcass Cymru, April 2018 (https://gov.wales/sites/default/files/publications/2018-05/review-of-research-and-case-law-on-parental-alienation.pdf), para. 4.4 at page 21 onwards, for an extensive overview of the research into this issue.

[48] Karen Woodall, 'World Health Organisation Recognises Parental Alienation', 27 May 2019, (https://karenwoodall.blog/2019/05/27/world-health-organisation-recognises-parental-alienation/)

[49] The Collective Memo of Concern to the World Health Organisation dated 10 July 2019 was signed by 352 family law academics, family violence experts, family

misuse to undermine the credibility of one parent alleging abuse as a reason for refusing contact. WHO subsequently clarified that the inclusion of the term for search purposes did not signify endorsement of the term or its use. After reconsidering its position, WHO also concluded that, as a result of it being an issue relevant to specific judicial contexts, its inclusion in the ICD-11 not contributing to health statistics, and there being no evidence-based health care interventions specifically for parental alienation, that in situations where an individual labelled with this term presents for health care, other ICD-11 content is sufficient to guide coding. As a result 'parental alienation' and its parallel index term 'parental estrangement' were removed from the ICD-11.[50]

WHO have also noted that it had decided not to include the concept and terminology of parental alienation in the classification itself, because it did not regard it as a health care term, noting that "*the term is rather used in legal contexts, generally in the context of custody disputes in divorce or other partnership dissolution.*"[51]

Different perspectives on parental alienation: does it really exist?

There is no doubt that some children inadvertently become, or are deliberately made to become, aligned to one parent at the expense of their relationship with the other. That is a well-known and accepted phenomenon. What frequently offends some psychiatrists and psychologists is the characterisation of this process or state as a syndrome. There is no such classification in the Diagnostic and Statistical Manual of Mental Disorders (DSM-5, since it is currently in its 5th revision), that lists mental health conditions recognised by the American Psychiatric Association, and WHO's position on its inclusion in the ICD-11 is outlined above. While there are a number of practitioners in the field of psychiatry and psychology who consider this to be a

violence research institutes, child development and child abuse experts, children's rights networks and associations, as well as 764 concerned individuals (https://www.learningtoendabuse.ca/docs/WHO-September-24-2019.pdf).

50 World Health Organisation (WHO), 'Parental alienation', https://www.who.int/standards/classifications/frequently-asked-questions/parental-alienation

51 ibid.

significant omission,[52] there are others who argue that there is insufficient research to validate its existence.

Furthermore, there is an argument which is gaining increasing attention: that allegations of parental alienation are being made in the context of cases which involve domestic abuse to challenge the legitimate objections of the abused parent to contact. In her 2020 article[53] Dr Adrienne Barnett concludes that:

> *"PA [parental alienation] is a concept that is proving more powerful than any other in silencing the voices of women and children resisting contact with abusive men. PA is not an 'equal' counterpart to domestic abuse, it is a means of obscuring domestic abuse, and should be recognised as such. We need to find 'other' ways of talking about children's welfare that recognise children's interlinked vulnerability, agency and relationships before any further harm is done to them."*

This issue will be discussed in detail in **Chapter 3: Parental alienation and domestic abuse**.

These are important considerations, but almost all commentators recognise that to undermine the relationship between a parent and a child without legitimate cause is a harmful and abusive act. The court must be alert to parents who engage in actions which cause that harm and proactively case manage those cases to avoid perpetuating or compounding the damage caused.

As noted by Parker J, first instance judge in the decision of in *Re H (Children)*[54]:

> *"I regard parental manipulation of children, of which I distressingly see an enormous amount, as exceptionally harmful. It distorts the relationship of the child not only with the parent but with the outside*

[52] William Bernet, M.D., *Parental Alienation, DSM-V and ICD-11,* American Series in Behavioural Science and Law. Charles C. Thomas Publisher, Ltd, Springfield, IL, 2010

[53] Adrienne Barnett, 'A genealogy of hostility: parental alienation in England and Wales', Journal of Social Welfare and Family Law, (2020) 42:1, 18-29

[54] [2014] EWCA Civ 733

world. Children who are suborned into flouting court orders are given extremely damaging messages about the extent to which authority can be disregarded and given the impression that compliance with adult expectations is optional. Bearing in mind the documented history of this mother's inability to control these children, their relationship with one another and wholly inappropriate empowerment, it strikes me as highly damaging in this case. I am disappointed that the professionals in this case are unable truly to understand this message. […] Parents who obstruct a relationship with the other parent are inflicting untold damage on their children and it is, in my view, about time that professionals truly understood this.'[55]

[55] ibid., para. 44

CHAPTER TWO

GENERAL PRINCIPLES REGARDING CONTACT

General principles

The introduction of section 1(2A) of the 1989 Act, inserted by section 11 of the Children and Families Act 2014 ('CFA 2014'), enshrined in statute the presumption that the involvement of both parents in the child's life will further the child's welfare (unless the contrary is shown). This is sometimes referred to as 'the presumption of parental involvement.'

Since the implementation of the 1989 Act and before the introduction of the CFA 2014, it was made clear by the court in a number of authorities that contact with a non-resident parent is fundamental to the welfare of a child and that it is important for a child to have a positive relationship with both parents.

Indeed, the message that an ongoing relationship with both parents was in a child's best interests should have already been understood prior to 2014 as a result of case law. In cases such as *Re O (Contact: imposition of conditions)*[56], the court had affirmed that, while the child's welfare is the paramount consideration of the court (as per section 1(1) of the 1989 Act), where parents were separated it was almost always in the child's interests to have contact with the other parent, as long as it was safe to do so, and only in infrequent cases would the court consider such contact should not be ordered. Where not ordered due to being unsafe, it was normally in the child's best interests for indirect contact to be maintained, provided it was not abused. The court made clear that the caring parent had reciprocal obligations, and an intransigent parent had no right to veto contact. The court emphasised its powers to enforce

[56] [1995] 2 FLR 124

orders for contact, which it can exercise if it was considered that it would promote a child's welfare.

This approach was endorsed by the court in *Re C (Direct Contact: Suspension)*[57] where the following principles relating to contact were outlined, providing a summary of the salient case law:

i. *"Contact between parent and child is a fundamental element of family life and is almost always in the interests of the child.*[58]

ii. *Contact between parent and child is to be terminated only in exceptional circumstances, where there are cogent reasons for doing so and when there is no alternative. Contact is to be terminated only if it will be detrimental to the child's welfare.*

iii. *There is a positive obligation on the State, and therefore on the judge, to take measures to maintain and to reconstitute the relationship between parent and child, in short, to maintain or restore contact. The judge has a positive duty to attempt to promote contact. The judge must grapple with all the available alternatives before abandoning hope of achieving some contact. He must be careful not to come to a premature decision, for contact is to be stopped only as a last resort and only once it has become clear that the child will not benefit from continuing the attempt.*

iv. *The court should take a medium-term and long-term view and not accord excessive weight to what appear likely to be short-term or transient problems.*

v. *The key question, which requires "stricter scrutiny", is whether the judge has taken all necessary steps to facilitate contact as can reasonably be demanded in the circumstances of the particular case.*

---

57 [2011] EWCA Civ 521

58 Note, as set out below, the subsequent amendment to section 1 Children Act 1989 in April 2014 which added sections 1(2A) and (2B), and a presumption that "unless the contrary is shown [...] involvement of that parent in the life of the child concerned will further the child's welfare."

vi. *All that said, at the end of the day the welfare of the child is paramount; "the child's interest must have precedence over any other consideration."*[59]

The above principles are essential, in particular in circumstances where it is being argued by a party, or considered by the court, that it may be appropriate to make an order that there is to be no direct contact taking place.

<u>The presumption of parental involvement</u>

As noted above, the promulgation of the CFA 2014 and the enactment of section 11, which brought about the introduction of sections 1(2A) and 1(2B) into the 1989 Act, now requires that where the court is considering a contested application to make, vary or discharge a child arrangements order pursuant to section 8 of the 1989 Act, it must, in relation to each parent, presume that involvement of that parent in the life of the child concerned will further that child's welfare, unless the contrary is shown.

As if by way of correction to the notion that there should be a presumption of equal or shared parenting, the statute reflects that the term 'involvement' "*means involvement of some kind, either direct or indirect, but not any particular division of a child's time*" (section 1(2B)).

It is important to acknowledge that the paramountcy of the child's welfare in determining any question with respect of a child's upbringing at section 1 of the 1989 Act is undiluted, and the statutory presumption does not change the fact that the other welfare factors within section 1(3) of the 1989 Act continue to be something the shall have regard to. This includes:

a. The ascertainable wishes and feelings of the child concerned (considered in light of his age and understanding);

b. Their physical, emotional and educational needs;

[59] *Re C (Direct Contact: Suspension)* [2011] EWCA Civ 521., para. 47

c. The likely effect on them of any change in their circumstances;

d. Their age, sex, background and any characteristics of them which the court considers relevant;

e. Any harm which they have suffered or are at risk of suffering;

f. How capable each of their parents, and any other person in relation to whom the court considers the question to be relevant, is of meeting their needs; and

g. The range of powers available to the court under the 1989 Act in the proceedings in question.

It should also be noted that the changes brought about by the CFA 2014 did not go as far as the recommendations in the interim report Family Justice Review report published in March 2011, chaired by David Norgrove.[60] The initial proposal was that there be a change in the legislature to enshrine in law a presumption of equal or shared parenting. Despite this, and a significant amount of lobbying, the final Family Justice Review report which followed in November 2011[61] ultimately concluded that there should be no such change in the legislation. In what is explained as a change engendered by the receipt of further evidence, the report states:

> *"The child's welfare should be the court's paramount consideration, as required by the Children Act 1989. No change should be made that might compromise this principle. Accordingly, no legislation should be introduced that creates or risks creating the perception that there is a parental right to substantially shared or equal time for both parents."*[62]

---

60 Family Justice Review Interim Report, March 2011 (https://assets.publishing.service.gov.uk/government/uploads/system/uploads/attachment_data/file/217357/family-justice-review-interim-rep.pdf)

61 Family Justice Review Final Report, November 2011 (https://assets.publishing.service.gov.uk/government/uploads/system/uploads/attachment_data/file/217343/family-justice-review-final-report.pdf),

62 ibid., para. 109

At that stage 'The Government Response to the Family Justice Review: A system with children and families at its heart'[63], set out the position as follows:

> *"59. The principle of continued shared parenting after separation underpins the approach which we have taken on private law. Both Governments believe that children benefit from both parents being as fully involved as possible in their child's upbringing, unless there are safety or welfare concerns.*
>
> *60. This is a sensitive issue with strong opinions on both sides of the debate. The Review decided to recommend no change in the law to establish a presumption of shared parenting, or to insert into legislation a statement about the need for a child to maintain a meaningful relationship with the parent who does not live with them. However, many people continue to have concerns about the proper recognition of the role of both parents by the courts.*
>
> *61. The Government believes that there should be a legislative statement of the importance of children having an ongoing relationship with both their parents after family separation, where that is safe, and in the child's best interests."*[64]

Following further consultation, the amendments were made reflecting that recommendation.

---

[63] Ministry of Justice and Department of Education, 'The Government Response to the Family Justice Review: A system with children and families at its heart', February 2012 (https://assets.publishing.service.gov.uk/government/uploads/system/uploads/attachment_data/file/177097/CM-8273.pdf)

[64] ibid.

The State's obligations

The UNCRC provides in Article 9[65]:

> *1. States Parties shall ensure that a child shall not be separated from his or her parents against their will, except when competent authorities subject to judicial review determine, in accordance with applicable law and procedures, that such separation is necessary for the best interests of the child. Such determination may be necessary in a particular case such as one involving abuse or neglect of the child by the parents, or one where the parents are living separately and a decision must be made as to the child's place of residence.*
>
> *2. In any proceedings pursuant to paragraph 1 of the present article, all interested parties shall be given an opportunity to participate in the proceedings and make their views known.*
>
> *3. States Parties shall respect the right of the child who is separated from one or both parents to maintain personal relations and direct contact with both parents on a regular basis, except if it is contrary to the child's best interests.*

Article 8 of the European Convention on Human Rights 1950 ('ECHR')[66] states that:

> *1. Everyone has the right to respect for his private and family life, his home and his correspondence.*
>
> *2. There shall be no interference by a public authority with the exercise of this right except such as is in accordance with the law and is necessary in a democratic society in the interests of national security, public safety or the economic well-being of the country, for the prevention of disorder or crime, for the protection of health or morals, or for the protection of the rights and freedoms of others.*

---

65 https://www.ohchr.org/en/instruments-mechanisms/instruments/convention-rights-child

66 https://www.legislation.gov.uk/ukpga/1998/42/schedule/1/part/I/chapter/7

A number of cases have explored the court's positive obligation to maintain or restore contact in the context of intractable contact disputes, in particular where this obligation begins and where it ends. This includes cases where it has been assessed to be in the child's best interests to continue trying to promote contact, and those where enforcement has been deemed contrary to the child's welfare. This also include cases where more robust methods such as transfer of residence, warship or an order for a section 37 investigation have been employed by the courts.

The starting point is found in *Re C (Direct Contact: Suspension)*, where, as observed above, the Court of Appeal concluded that the State and the court have a positive obligation to promote contact and to take steps and adopt strategies to maintain and to re-establish a relationship between parent and child where it has become attenuated. The judge must explore alternatives in the quest to repair the relationship between parent and child. Direct contact, or indeed contact in any form, is to be stopped only as a last resort, once any benefit to the child is manifestly outweighed by the disadvantages it will bring.

In *Re A (A Child)*[67], the Court of Appeal was concerned with a father's appeal against an order that his fourteen year old daughter should have no direct contact with him. His appeal was successful. The Court of Appeal held that while the wishes and feelings of the child would be important in some cases in determining what order was in the child's welfare, and in some cases determinative, a parent's implacable hostility should rarely deter a court from ordering contact where the child's welfare otherwise required it. The court was particularly concerned with the fact that human rights violations might also arise from a refusal of direct contact, and that contact should only be refused where the court is satisfied that a risk of harm exists if ordered. The Court of Appeal concluded that the court at first instance should have taken a much tougher approach by ensuring adverse consequences resulted from non-compliance with orders. The court had failed in its responsibility to enforce its own orders and it had extensive powers to do so. The trial judge's analysis was also deficient, in particular the weight that had been given to the child's wishes and feelings in the context of their views on

[67] [2013] EWCA Civ 1104

contact having been inconsistently expressed. McFarlane LJ (as he then was), noted:

> *"This decision is made with a heavy heart as I fully understand that the idea of re-opening these matters before the court will be a profoundly unwelcome one for M [the child]. That it is necessary, for the reasons that I have given, I am clear, just as I am clear that, on this rare occasion, part of the responsibility for this turn of events rests with those of us who work in the Family Justice system. But sight must not be lost of the place where the ultimate responsibility for this situation plainly rests, which is with the parents and, in this case, with M's mother in particular. It is she who has, on the judge's clear and unchallenged findings, doggedly refused to allow M to develop and maintain a relationship with her father without any good reason whatsoever for so doing; it is she, should she wish to do so, who could now unlock this intractable situation and permit her daughter to have some form of normality and balance in her relationship with her parents as she goes through her teenage years and beyond."*[68]

In a different context *Re A (Children) (Contact: Ultra-Orthodox Judaism: Transgender Parent)*[69] was a decision in which the issue was whether a transgendered parent should have contact with her children, who were all living within the ultra-orthodox Jewish community with their mother. The Court of Appeal gave an insight into the lengths the State must go in promoting contact, and considered that Peter Jackson J (as he then was) had given up too soon. Sir James Munby, the then PFD, stated:

> *"In our judgment, the best interests of these children seen in the medium to longer term is in more contact with their father if that can be achieved. So strong are the interests of the children in the eyes of the law that the courts must, with respect to the learned judge, persevere. As the law says in other contexts, "never say never". To repeat, the doors should not be closed at this early stage in their lives."*[70]

---

68 ibid., para. 78

69 [2017] EWCA Civ 2164

70 ibid., para. 138

In so saying, an analogy was drawn to a situation involving cases where there was an implacably hostile parent and where the court adopted a robust approach to the question of contact.

The message is that the court has to exhaust all reasonable options, as Williams J made clear in *Re R (A Child: Appeal: Termination of Contact).*[71] Peter Jackson LJ has since affirmed this message in the Court of Appeal in *Re S (Parental Alienation: Cult)*[72]:

> *"In summary, in a situation of parental alienation the obligation on the court is to respond with exceptional diligence and take whatever effective measures are available. The situation calls for judicial resolve because the line of least resistance is likely to be less stressful for the child and for the court in the short term. But it does not represent a solution to the problem. Inaction will probably reinforce the position of the stronger party at the expense of the weaker party and the bar will be raised for the next attempt at intervention. Above all, the obligation on the court is to keep the child's medium to long term welfare at the forefront of its mind and wherever possible to uphold the child and parent's right to respect for family life before it is breached. In making its overall welfare decision the court must therefore be alert to early signs of alienation. What will amount to effective action will be a matter of judgement, but it is emphatically not necessary to wait for serious, worse still irreparable, harm to be done before appropriate action is taken. It is easier to conclude that decisive action was needed after it has become too late to take it."*[73]

Welfare

The unambiguous duty of the court to promote contact is subject to the need for there to be a holistic welfare evaluation in each case, and, neither the obligation, nor the powers of the court are limitless.

While the welfare of the child concerned is paramount (section 1(1) of the 1989 Act), how to attain an outcome that achieves the appropriate

---

71 [2019] EWHC 132 (Fam)

72 [2020] EWCA Civ 568

73 ibid. para. 13

balance is not straightforward since the issues are complex and means of addressing parental alienation are themselves controversial.

As Peter Jackson LJ adverted to in the above quote from *Re S (Parental Alienation: Cult)*, the question of child's welfare is often not straightforward in cases where a child has been alienated from his or her parent. In such cases the issue of welfare has to be considered with an eye to both the present and the future. The court may use its powers to interrupt a pattern or intervene to end a destructive dynamic in order to avert foreseeable and anticipated harm. However, the immediate consequences of doing so will need to be considered and balanced.

The court is required to consider each of the aspects of the 'welfare checklist' pursuant to section 1(3) of the 1989 Act, but how is the court to evaluate the question of best interests in cases of high conflict and significant hostility? In *Re A (Children) (Contact: Ultra-Orthodox Judaism: Transgender Parent)* it was said that there is a need for the court to act as a "*judicially reasonable parent*" by "*judging the child's welfare by the standards of reasonable men and women today, 2017 [...] always remembering that the reasonable man or woman is receptive to change, broadminded, tolerant, easy-going and slow to condemn.*"[74] The need to consider each case as a judicially reasonable parent would will apply no less to cases involving intractable contact disputes, including those involving a hostile parent, where the court will be required to navigate its way through complex relational crosswinds in order to come to the right best interests decision for the child concerned.

This will mean considering all factors in the welfare checklist in the association with each other, but also in the context of the factual matrix and prevailing family dynamics in relation to each realistic outcome for the subject child.

[74] [2017] EWCA Civ 216, ibid., para. 60

Wishes and feelings

In a case where there are allegations of parental alienation, the consideration of the child's wishes and feelings may be particularly complicated. In *Re D (A Child) (Abduction: Rights of Custody)*[75], Baroness Hale considered that:

> *"As any parent who has ever asked a child what he wants for tea knows, there is a large difference between taking account of a child's views and doing what he wants. Especially in Hague Convention cases, the relevance of the child's views to the issues in the case may be limited. But there is now a growing understanding of the importance of listening to the children involved in children's cases. It is the child, more than anyone else, who will have to live with what the court decides. Those who do listen to children understand that they often have a point of view which is quite distinct from that of the person looking after them. They are quite capable of being moral actors in their own right. Just as the adults may have to do what the court decides whether they like it or not, so may the child. But that is no more a reason for failing to hear what the child has to say than it is for refusing to hear the parent's views."*[76]

However, as noted above, the question of the significance and importance of the wishes and feelings of the subject child is complicated in cases of alleged implacable hostility. As Jackson J (as he then was) stated in *Re M (Contact)*[77]:

> *"...it is important to distinguish between real wishes and feelings on one hand, and statements that the children make, and think they mean, on the other. Having considered the matter carefully, I am convinced that these children love their father and want to be able to see him, but that they are being prevented from showing those feelings or acting on them."*[78]

---

75 [2006] UKHL 51

76 ibid., para. 57

77 [2012] EWHC 1948 (Fam)

78 ibid., para. 61

Parker J's words, as quoted by the Court of Appeal when it upheld her decision in *Re H (Children)*[79], are apposite:

> *"I have more than once stressed in this case, as in others, that the word used in the Children Act about wishes and feelings is "ascertainable" and not "expressed". "Ascertainable" often means that the Court has to look at actions rather than words. The ascertainable wishes and feelings of these boys have been demonstrated by the evidence that they are more than happy to be with their father."*[80]

This theme will be explored in greater depth in **Chapter 6: The voice of the child**.

For the moment it is sufficient to note that it is not the case, even where a court finds alienation has occurred and that the child's wishes and feelings are likely not their own, that the court will necessarily continue in its attempts to promote contact. Welfare requires a balance to be struck between continuing attempts to get contact up and running, and the wider harm that this may cause to a child.

In *Re Q (A Child) (Implacable contact dispute)*[81], at a first instance review hearing in a long-running contact dispute, HHJ Brasse departed from the strategy of seeking to order contact after a number of unsuccessful attempts. During the proceedings, it had been found that allegations against the father were false, and that the child had been influenced by the mother's hostility towards the father. Nonetheless, at the hearing a number of options, including making a child arrangements order and directing the local authority to produce a section 37 report, were dismissed. The only order that was made was a specific issues order that the child attend therapy. The father's appeal was unsuccessful. Whilst *Re C (A Child) (Direct Contact Suspension)* was considered, and in particular the positive obligation on the court to promote contact, the Court of Appeal concluded that HHJ Brasse's decision was not only open to him to take but the only path that would increase the prospect of contact in the future. As ordering contact had simply failed in the past, there was

---

[79] [2014] EWCA Civ 733

[80] ibid., para. 43

[81] [2015] EWCA Civ 991

no reason to believe it would be successful thereon. The judge was engaging with non-court methods to facilitate future contact; the r.16.4 guardian and a clinic had both advised the only option was therapy but it could not begin while proceedings continued. Sir James Munby, then PFD, ended the judgment with the following stark warning to the mother:

> *"I would not want the mother to think she has won. She has not. There are no winners here, only losers. Q is far and away the greatest loser – and that, in overwhelming measure, is because of his mother's behaviour. I urge her again, as I urged her during the hearing, to reflect on Judge Brasse's findings. They are an indictment of her parental failings hitherto. She, and Q, now stand at the cross-roads. It is vital, absolutely vital, that she participates, with Q and with the father, in the therapy which is at present their only hope for a happy future. I repeat what I said during the hearing. Sooner or later, and probably sooner than she would hope, Q will discover the truth – the truth about why he is not seeing his father, the truth about the harm his mother has done to him, the truth about his father, the truth that his father is not the monster he has been brought up to believe he is, the truth about, and the dreadful details of, the litigation. When he discovers that truth, what is his mother going to be able to say to him? How is she going to begin to justify her behaviour? She needs to think very carefully about how she is going to handle that day, not if but when it comes. Whatever she may think about the father, does she really want to imperil her future relationship with her son? Run the risk of being disowned by him? Run the risk of never seeing her own grandchildren? I urge her to think, long and hard, and to act before it is too late."*[82]

Similarly, in *Re J (Children)*[83] the Court of Appeal dismissed an appeal against a trial judge's decision to not order contact in line with the recommendation of the guardian's view that the child's views were too entrenched, holding that it was contrary to the children's welfare interests to contemplate a re-hearing.

---

[82] ibid. para. 31

[83] [2018] EWCA Civ 115

The holistic welfare balancing exercise

A more detailed analysis of the different options available to the court to give effect to the obligation to promote contact will be discussed in the following Chapters. For the purposes of this Chapter, it is sufficient to mention the comments of Ryder LJ in the Court of Appeal decision of *Re F (A Child) (International Relocation Case)* is instructive.[84] In this decision, the Court of Appeal confirmed that the holistic welfare balancing exercise applies just as much to private law cases as it does to public law cases, and gave the following guidance:

> *"28. Given the agreement of the parties to an holistic approach to the court's welfare analysis, I need to set out what that involves. The re-crafting of section 8 orders from residence and contact into child arrangements orders has inter alia the benefit of emphasising, absent adverse circumstances and welfare conclusions, the equality of parental responsibility that each parent has. Parents are to be expected to exercise their autonomy and to respect the autonomy of their children by entering into arrangements that plan for their children's long term welfare by providing for a meaningful relationship between each adult and each child. Where they cannot agree there is likely to be more than one proposal for the court to consider.*
>
> *29. In Re W (Care Plans) [2013] EWCA Civ 1227, [2014] 2 FLR 431 at [76 — 78] I held that in relation to public law children proceedings the welfare analysis of realistic options that is required would be facilitated by a balancing exercise first recommended by Thorpe LJ in the different context of a medical treatment case in Re A (Male Sterilisation) [2000] 1 FLR 549 at 560. That approach had been identified by my Lord, McFarlane LJ in Re G (Care Proceedings: Welfare Evaluation) [2013] EWCA Civ 965, [2014] 1 FLR 670 at [54]:*
>
> > *"What is required is a balancing exercise in which each option is evaluated to the degree of detail necessary to analyse and weigh its*

[84] [2015] EWCA Civ 882

own internal positives and negatives and each option is then compared, side by side, against the competing option or options."

It was subsequently approved by Sir James Munby P in this court in Re B-S (Children) [2013] EWCA Civ 1146, [2014] 1 FLR 1935 at [36] and at [46] where the approach was described by him in these terms:

"We emphasise the words 'global, holistic evaluation'. This point is crucial. The judicial task is to evaluate <u>all</u> the options, undertaking a global, holistic and ... multi-faceted evaluation of the child's welfare which takes into account <u>all</u> the negatives and the positives, <u>all</u> the pros and cons, of <u>each</u> option"

30. That approach is no more than a reiteration of good practice. Where there is more than one proposal before the court, a welfare analysis of each proposal will be necessary. That is neither a new approach nor is it an option. A welfare analysis is a requirement in any decision about a child's upbringing. The sophistication of that analysis will depend on the facts of the case. Each realistic option for the welfare of a child should be validly considered on its own internal merits (i.e. an analysis of the welfare factors relating to each option should be undertaken). That prevents one option (often in a relocation case the proposals from the absent or 'left behind' parent) from being sidelined in a linear analysis. Not only is it necessary to consider both parents' proposals on their own merits and by reference to what the child has to say but it is also necessary to consider the options side by side in a comparative evaluation. A proposal that may have some but no particular merit on its own may still be better than the only other alternative which is worse."

CHAPTER THREE

PARENTAL ALIENATION AND DOMESTIC ABUSE

It is perhaps unsurprising that the interrelationship between allegations of domestic abuse and those of parental alienation have remained at the centre of an increasingly polarised debate. The pages of law reports and academic journals are filled with arguments directed at this thorny issue.

Following the report of Glaser and Sturges[85] referred to in *Re L, Re V, Re M, Re H (Contact: Domestic Violence),*[86] and its analysis and categorisation of the different reasons for a child's rejection of their parent, it might be thought that the identification of the various potential sources of that rejection would have paved the way for a more nuanced discussion of the forces at play in circumstances where a child is becoming, or has become, estranged from a parent. While the Glaser and Sturges' report continues to inform the work of those practising in this field, there has been a growing focus on the concern that what may be framed as parental alienation is, in reality, the genuine and legitimate response of a child to domestic abuse, whether in the form of coercive and controlling behaviour or otherwise. Of course, such an explanation may be considered entirely congruent with the observations made by those two experts, but the debate now frequently elides one explanation at the expense of the other.

On one side of the divide it is argued that parental alienation is a construct which is too often deployed to meet authentic allegations of domestic abuse. This line of academic debate has existed for some time, Meier in 2009 argued that parental alienation claims can be "*far more often used in practice to deny real abuse than to actually reduce psychological*

[85] Drs Glaser and Sturges, 'Contact and domestic violence: the experts court report', [2000] Fam Law 615

[86] [2000] EWCA Civ 194

harm to children."[87] The abstract of an article by Dr Adrienne Barnett[88] engages with that issue in the following way:

> *"A clear pattern emerged of, initially, parental alienation syndrome and subsequently PA [parental alienation] being raised in family proceedings and in political and popular arenas in response to concerns about and measures to address domestic abuse. The case law revealed a high incidence of domestic abuse perpetrated by parents (principally fathers) who were claiming that the resident parents (principally mothers) had alienated the children against them, which raises questions about the purpose of PA."*

The suggestion advanced by Barnett is that there is a danger that parents (usually mothers) who have been the victims of domestic abuse are cast as alienating parents, and the response to the issue of contact is driven by inappropriate hostility to the other parent rather than legitimate fear for themselves or their children.

In its 2018 report,[89] written in partnership with Queen Mary University, Women's Aid argued, when considering the interface between allegations of domestic abuse and those of parental alienation, that:

> *"...the evidence collected as part of this research illustrates many examples of gendered myths, stereotypes, attitudes and behaviours around survivors and perpetrators of domestic abuse that lie within the deep structure of the family court system. Use of parental alienation accusations against women who raise domestic abuse and their concerns*

---

87 J.S. Meir, 'A Historical Perspective on Parental Alienation Syndrome and Parental Alienation', Journal of Child Custody, (2009) 6(3-4), 250

88 Dr Adrienne Barnett 'A genealogy of hostility: parental alienation in England and Wales', Journal of Social Welfare and Family Law, (2020) 42:1, 18-29. Also see Dr Adrienne Barnett's article for Women's Aid, 'Parental alienation and the family courts', 28 April 2020, (https://www.womensaid.org.uk/parental-alienation-and-the-family-courts/)

89 Jenny Birchall and Professor Shazia Choudhry, Women's Aid & Queen Mary University, (2018), 'What about my right not to be abused? Domestic Abuse, Human Rights and the Family Courts,' (https://www.womensaid.org.uk/wp-content/uploads/2018/05/Domestic-abuse-human-rights-and-the-family-courts-report.pdf)

around unsafe contact between their child(ren) and the perpetrator of the abuse are one of the most extreme examples of this."[90]

There are those who further contend that allegations of parental alienation are made as a form, or continuation of, abusive behaviour, and the court process is being subverted to license that conduct.

Equally, the June 2020 report by the Ministry of Justice's Harm Panel[91] critiques what it labels a "*pro-contact culture*" in the family court, and speaks of the need for a culture shift in terms of the perception and treatment of domestic abuse in private law cases:

> *"The evidence submitted to the panel suggested that the pro-contact culture results in a pattern of minimisation and disbelief of allegations of domestic abuse and child sexual abuse [...] the evidence suggesting that domestic abuse may be treated as 'historic' to enable contact to occur, rather than considering whether abuse has ongoing relevance to the welfare of the child and non abusive parent. We also explore the evidence as to how allegations of domestic abuse can sometimes be reformulated as mutual 'high conflict' or, increasingly, used by the other parent as evidence of 'parental alienation'. While parents alleging domestic abuse told the panel that they felt that they were regarded as obstructive, they also felt that abusive parents were generally given the benefit of the doubt and awarded contact without evidence of change."*[92]

---

90 ibid., page 36

91 The Ministry of Justice's Harm Panel, 'Assessing Risk of Harm to Children and Parents in Private Law Children Cases' (June 2020) (https://consult.justice.gov.uk/digital-communications/assessing-harm-private-family-law-proceedings/results/assessing-risk-harm-children-parents-pl-childrens-cases-report.pdf)

92 Ibid., page 43. See also 'Improving the family court response to domestic abuse: Proposals for a mechanism to monitor and report on domestic abuse in private law children proceedings' (November 2021) produced by the victims commissioner and the domestic abuse commissioner in the wake of the Harm Panel report.

On the other side of the debate, there are those who argue that parental alienation is a form of child abuse.[93] Indeed, parental alienation of a child is a form of direct psychological and emotional abuse of the child, and will therefore fall directly under the definition of domestic abuse featured in PD12J.[94] It can also be considered a form of coercive and controlling or abusive behaviour on the part of the parent who is actively manipulating the situation to continue to punish or dominate their former partner through control of their child.[95] A report published by Parental Alienation UK concludes that parental alienation is "*a devasting form of family violence where psychological abuse and coercive control is at its heart.*"[96]

It is clear therefore that cases involving allegations of domestic abuse frequently also involve allegations or counter-allegations of parental alienation. From the vantage point of the parent alleging abuse, the child's objections are legitimate and justified as a result of the abuser's conduct. From the perspective of the parent alleging alienation, the allegations are fabricated or exaggerated, and serve as further evidence of the parent's hostile position and alienation.

---

93 Baker, A. J. L., (2020), 'Parental alienation and empirical research' in D. Lorandos and William Bernet (eds.), *Parental Alienation: Science and Law,* pp. 207-253. Springfield, IL: Charles C Thomas Publisher

94 Practice Direction 12J, para. 2A

95 Nick Woodall, 'The Role of Domestic Violence in Parental Alienation', 5 April 2016, (https://www.nickwoodall.net/articles/); Karen Woodall, 'Coercive control in cases of alienation of children in divorce and separation', 14 April 2021, (https://karenwoodall.blog/2021/04/14/coercive-control-in-cases-of-alienation-of-children-in-divorce-and-separation/); Hamberger, L. K., Larsen, S. E., & Lehrner, A., (2017), 'Coercive control in intimate partner violence', *Aggression & Violence Behavior,* 37, 1-1

96 'The UK Parental Alienation Study 2020' (https://parentalalienationuk.info/our-report/)

Defining domestic abuse

Domestic abuse is defined in the Domestic Abuse Act 2021 as behaviour of a person ('A') towards another person ('B') if A and B are each aged 16 or over and are personally connected[97] to each other and the behaviour is abusive (section 1(2)).

Behaviour is considered 'abusive' if it consists of physical or sexual abuse; violent or threatening behaviour; controlling or coercive behaviour; economic abuse, or psychological, emotional or other abuse. It does not matter whether the behaviour consists of a single incident or a course of conduct (section 1(3)).

The Act makes clear however that A's behaviour may be behaviour 'towards' B despite the fact that it consists of conduct directed at another person (for example, B's child) (section 1(5)).

The Act also specifically makes provision for children as victims of abuse. This includes circumstances where the behaviour of a person ('A') towards another person ('B') is domestic abuse (section 3(1)). Any reference includes a reference to a child who (a) sees or hears, or experiences the effects of, the abuse, and, (b) is related to A or B (section 3(2)). A child is related to a person for the purposes of section 3(2) if (a) the person is a parent of, or has parental responsibility for, the child, or (b) the child and the person are relatives (section 3(3)).

The above definition has now been incorporated into PD12J. The Practice Direction also provides definitions for coercive and controlling behaviour, as follows[98]:

> "coercive behaviour" means an act or a pattern of acts of assault, threats, humiliation and intimidation or other abuse that is used to harm, punish or frighten the victim.
>
> "controlling behaviour" means an act or pattern of acts designed to make a person subordinate and/or dependent by isolating them

97 Defined in the Domestic Abuse Act 2021, section 2.

98 PD12J, para. 3

from sources of support, exploiting their resources and capacities for personal gain, depriving them of the means needed for independent, resistance and escape and regulating their everyday behaviour.

It is acknowledged as part of PD12J that domestic abuse is harmful to children, and/or puts children at risk of harm, including where they are victims of domestic abuse for example by witnessing one of their parents being violent to the other, or living in a home in which domestic abuse is perpetrated (even if the child is too young to be conscious of the behaviour). Children may suffer direct physical, psychological and/or emotional harm from living with and being victims of domestic abuse, and may also suffer harm indirectly where the domestic abuse impairs the parenting capacity of either or both of their parents.[99]

<u>The necessity of determining the factual matrix</u>

The recent focus on coercive and controlling behaviour as a form of abuse[100] has added to the challenges facing lawyers and judges, with an acknowledged need to disentangle the two frequently related but different issues of domestic abuse and parental alienation.

Whilst the allegations on each side of a contact dispute may be different, the initial case management of proceedings where there are competing allegations is very much the same. In each case the court will have to ask itself whether the allegations have substance and are germane to the child arrangements for the relevant child and questions related to contact: its

99 PD12J, para. 4. "Harm" is defined at para. 3 as meaning ill-treatment or the impairment of health or development including, for example, impairment suffered from being a victim of domestic abuse or from seeing or hearing the ill-treatment of another, by way of domestic abuse or otherwise.

100 The case of *F v M* [2021] EWFC 4 provides a lucid and authoritative exposition on the how controlling and coercive behaviour can be defined and identified, which was expressly endorsed by the Court of Appeal in *Re H-N and Others (children) (domestic abuse: finding of fact hearings)* [2021] EWCA Civ 448 at paragraph 51, commenting *"it follows that consideration of whether the evidence establishes an abusive pattern of coercive and/or controlling behaviour is likely to be the primary question in many cases where there is an allegation of domestic abuse, irrespective of whether there are other more specific factual allegations to be determined."*

form, frequency and safety. However, the court must also be alert to what may be more subtle issues in respect of the dynamic of the relationship, and how this may impact on contact or a child's attitude to contact.

The way the court frequently deals with this is to list a fact-finding hearing at which the factual matrix is determined in advance of any welfare decision being made. The need for fact-finding hearings is not limited to instances where there are allegations of domestic abuse and applies to situations where there are allegations or factual disputes which need to be determined.

Early determination of the facts

In the case of a parent alleging parental alienation the court has been very clear that an early evaluation of the validity of that contention is as important as determining whether allegation of domestic abuse are well founded.

As noted by Munby J (as he then was) in *Re D (Intractable Contact Dispute: Publicity)*[101]:

> *"The court should grasp the nettle … allegations should be speedily investigated and resolved, not left to fester unresolved and a continuing source of friction and dispute. Court time must be found — and found without delay —for fact finding hearings. Judges must resist the temptation to delay the evil day in the hope that perhaps the problem will go away."*[102]

In his more recent keynote address to the Families Need Fathers Conference in 2018, Munby LJ (as he then was), commented:

> *"The Women's Aid research describes accusations of parental alienation being used against women who raise concerns about domestic abuse to the extent that allegations of abuse are "obscured by allegations of parental alienation against the non-abusive parent."*

[101] [2004] EWHC 727 (Fam)

[102] ibid., para. 54

Drawing matters together, that short quotation from the Women's Aid research neatly points to a theme in this short address which is to stress the importance of fact finding. It is, as I have already observed crucial, both to the interests of the alleged victim and, in fact, to those of the alleged perpetrator, for any significant allegations of domestic abuse to be investigated and determined as matters of fact, similarly any significant allegation of "alienation," should also be laid out before the court and, if possible, determined on the same basis."[103]

Similarly, HHJ Wildblood QC notes in *Re A (Children) (Parental alienation)*[104]:

"[...] At no point prior to my involvement in 2017 was there a full hearing on evidence to determine what was going on in this family. There were underlying and important allegations of fact that needed to be resolved but my comment is not limited to the absence of a fact-finding hearing. In my opinion, it was essential that there should be a definitive judgment explaining the difficulties within this family so that future work with the family members could be based upon that judgment."[105]

In short, the court will be unable to determine the prism through which the court manages the rest of the proceedings, in particular how it responds to the child's wishes and feelings (see **Chapter 6: The voice of the child**), without determining the veracity of competing allegations. In any event, the factual matrix will need to be determined before a section 7 report is ordered. As noted by McFarlane LJ (as he then was) in *Re J (Children) (Contact Orders: Procedure)*[106]:

"As paragraph 22 of the current version of PD12J advises, it is not usual for a s 7 welfare report to be ordered prior to any fact-finding hearing being concluded. It is obvious that this should be so; where

[103] Lord Justice McFarlane, 'Families Need Fathers Conference 2018 – Keynote Address by Lord Justice McFarlane', 25 June 2018 (https://www.judiciary.uk/wp-content/uploads/2018/06/speech-lj-mcfarlane-fnf.pdf)

[104] [2019] 9 WLUK 445

[105] ibid., para. 13(iv)

[106] [2018] EWCA Civ 115

there is a polarised factual dispute, how can the report writer form an informed view on welfare. In the present case, at its extreme, the welfare reporter would need to know if the children had been exposed to a sustained pattern of domestic abuse emanating from their father, or, conversely, whether the mother had manipulated the children so as to alienate them from an otherwise loving parent."[107]

<u>PD12J (Child Arrangements & Contact Orders: Domestic Abuse and Harm)</u>

Given how intertwined allegations of parental alienation and domestic abuse can be, it is important to consider the role of PD12J in determining whether the latter has taken place as opposed to or, possibly as well as, the former. PD12B makes clear that that in the context of application for child arrangements that *"if the court considers that a fact-finding hearing is necessary it shall conduct that hearing in accordance with revised Practice Direction 12J."*[108]

So, what is PD12J? Paragraph 2 of PD12J states as follows:

> *"The purpose of this Practice Direction is to set out what the Family Court or the High Court is required to do in any case in which it is alleged or admitted, or there is other reason to believe, that the child or a party has experienced domestic abuse perpetrated by another party or that there is a risk of such abuse."*

The context of this Practice Direction is that the starting point for any court is that child's welfare will ordinarily be best served by the involvement of a parent in that child's life. That is both the effect of statute[109] and the implication of case law. However, it came to be considered that there was an overemphasis on the need to establish or maintain contact and lack of emphasis upon the safety of the resident parent. The reframing of PD12J was intended to redress that balance:

---

[107] ibid., para. 84

[108] Practice Direction 12B, para. 20.1

[109] Children Act 1989, section 1(2A), as discussed in detail in **Chapter 2: General principles regarding contact.**

"...the involvement of a parent in a child's life will further the child's welfare, unless there is evidence to the contrary. The court must in every case consider carefully whether the statutory presumption applies, having particular regard to any allegation or admission of harm by domestic abuse to the child or parent or any evidence indicating such harm or risk of harm."[110]

Thus, what is called and framed as the statutory presumption can be displaced in the event that there is a risk of harm to the child of such a nature as to outweigh the presumed welfare benefits of the involvement of that parent.[111]

As a function of PD12J, the Family Court is required to consider the impact and relevance of allegations domestic abuse in the context of child arrangement cases.[112] PD12J envisages that there may be occasions when the assumption that contact should take place is nullified by the risk or potential risk arising from domestic abuse both at an interim or final stage. This necessarily engages with the question of whether allegations are raised as an obstruction to contact or they are a legitimate reason for denying it or arranging it in such a way as it ensures the safety of the child and other parent.

The question that was recently posed in the case of *Re H-N and Others (children) (domestic abuse: finding of fact hearings)*[113] was whether, in the light of a number of controversial judgments, including the four Judgments which were being appealed, PD12J remains fit for purpose. The Court of Appeal in *Re H-N* concluded, in answer to this question:

"... PD12J is and remains, fit for the purpose for which it was designed namely to provide the courts with a structure enabling the court first to recognise all forms of domestic abuse and thereafter on how to approach such allegations when made in private law proceedings. As

[110] PD12J, para. 7

[111] Despite this, some still argue that there appears to have been a dogged adherence to the notion that contact is best the findings of the Ministry of Justice's Harm Panel report (June 2020), as noted above.

[112] Practice Direction 12J, paragraph 1

[113] [2021] EWCA Civ 448

was also recognised by The Harm Panel, we are satisfied that the structure properly reflects modern concepts and understanding of domestic abuse. The challenge relates to the proper implementation of PD12J."[114]

There are factual disputes in almost all applications under section 8 of the 1989 Act, and there are almost invariably claims made on each side about the other's conduct. A proportion of what is alleged may require determination, although that might appropriately await a final hearing. In any event, the Court of Appeal's judgment makes it plain that not all negative or hostile behaviour which is perceived by one party to be abusive will be considered by the court to be so. It will not necessarily be in all cases that a standalone fact-finding hearing is considered necessary. As the Court of Appeal stated:

> *"It is equally important to be clear that not all directive, assertive, stubborn or selfish behaviour, will be 'abuse' in the context of proceedings concerning the welfare of a child; much will turn on the intention of the perpetrator of the alleged abuse and on the harmful impact of the behaviour. We would endorse the approach taken by Peter Jackson LJ in Re L (Relocation: Second Appeal) [2017] EWCA Civ 2121 (paragraph 61):*
>
>> *"Few relationships lack instances of bad behaviour on the part of one or both parties at some time and it is a rare family case that does not contain complaints by one party against the other, and often complaints are made by both. Yet not all such behaviour will amount to 'domestic abuse', where 'coercive behaviour' is defined as behaviour that is 'used to harm, punish, or frighten the victim...' and 'controlling behaviour' as behaviour 'designed to make a person subordinate...' In cases where the alleged behaviour does not have this character it is likely to be unnecessary and disproportionate for detailed findings of fact to be made about the complaints; indeed, in such cases it will not be in the interests of*

[114] ibid., para 28

the child or of justice for the court to allow itself to become another battleground for adult conflict."[115]

However, where the allegations of domestic abuse, in all its forms, are made, the Court of Appeal emphasises the need for the court to evaluate whether a fact-finding hearing is necessary using PD12J as a guide:

> *"The court will carefully consider the totality of PD12J, but to summarise, the proper approach to deciding if a fact-finding hearing is necessary is, we suggest, as follows:*
>
> *i. The first stage is to consider the nature of the allegations and the extent to which it is likely to be relevant in deciding whether to make a child arrangements order and if so in what terms (PD12J.5).*
>
> *ii. In deciding whether to have a finding of fact hearing the court should have in mind its purpose (PD12J.16) which is, in broad terms, to provide a basis of assessment of risk and therefore the impact of the alleged abuse on the child or children.*
>
> *iii. Careful consideration must be given to PD12J.17 as to whether it is 'necessary' to have a finding of fact hearing, including whether there is other evidence which provides a sufficient factual basis to proceed and importantly, the relevance to the issue before the court if the allegations are proved.*
>
> *iv. Under PD12J.17(h) the court has to consider whether a separate fact-finding hearing is 'necessary and proportionate'. The court and the parties should have in mind as part of its analysis both the overriding objective and the President's Guidance as set out in 'The Road Ahead.'"*[116]

---

[115] ibid., para. 32

[116] ibid. para. 37

It is clear from the Court of Appeal's guidance that it remains essential therefore to have full regard to Practice Direction 12J at paragraphs 5, 16 and 17 in determining the need for and scope of a fact-finding in relation to case where domestic abuse is alleged:

> *5. The court must, at all stages of the proceedings, and specifically at the First Hearing Dispute Resolution Appointment ('FHDRA'), consider whether domestic abuse is raised as an issue, either by the parties or by Cafcass or Cafcass Cymru or otherwise, and if so must –*
>
> - *identify at the earliest opportunity (usually at the FHDRA) the factual and welfare issues involved;*
> - *consider the nature of any allegation, admission or evidence of domestic abuse, and the extent to which it would be likely to be relevant in deciding whether to make a child arrangements order and, if so, in what terms;*
> - *give directions to enable contested relevant factual and welfare issues to be tried as soon as possible and fairly;*
> - *ensure that where domestic abuse is admitted or proven, any child arrangements order in place protects the safety and wellbeing of the child and the parent with whom the child is living, and does not expose either of them to the risk of further harm; and*
> - *ensure that any interim child arrangements order (i.e. considered by the court before determination of the facts, and in the absence of admission) is only made having followed the guidance in paragraphs 25–27 below.*
>
> *In particular, the court must be satisfied that any contact ordered with a parent who has perpetrated domestic abuse does not expose the child and/or other parent to the risk of harm and is in the best interests of the child. […]*

16. The court should determine as soon as possible whether it is necessary to conduct a fact-finding hearing in relation to any disputed allegation of domestic abuse –

a. in order to provide a factual basis for any welfare report or for assessment of the factors set out in paragraphs 36 and 37 below;

b. in order to provide a basis for an accurate assessment of risk;

c. before it can consider any final welfare-based order(s) in relation to child arrangements; or

d. before it considers the need for a domestic abuse-related Activity (such as a Domestic Violence Perpetrator Programme (DVPP)).

17. In determining whether it is necessary to conduct a fact-finding hearing, the court should consider –

a. the views of the parties and of Cafcass or CAFCASS Cymru;

b. whether there are admissions by a party which provide a sufficient factual basis on which to proceed;

c. if a party is in receipt of legal aid, whether the evidence required to be provided to obtain legal aid provides a sufficient factual basis on which to proceed;

d. whether there is other evidence available to the court that provides a sufficient factual basis on which to proceed;

e. whether the factors set out in paragraphs 36 and 37 below can be determined without a fact-finding hearing;

f. the nature of the evidence required to resolve disputed allegations;

g. whether the nature and extent of the allegations, if proved, would be relevant to the issue before the court; and h. *whether a separate fact-finding hearing would be necessary and proportionate in all the circumstances of the case.*

The same sorts of considerations should come into play in respect of allegations of parental alienation, particularly where one side of the narrative frames the parent child relationship in the context of domestic abuse and the counter-narrative offers an account of a disrupted relationship which arises from parental alienation.

It should be noted however that in the recent Court of Appeal decision of *K v K*[117], Sir Geoffrey Vos attempted to refine the approach in *Re H-N*, and emphasised that a "*decision to hold a fact-finding hearing is a major judicial determination within the course of family proceedings*" that will lead to delay, postponement of interim determination of issues and a likely deterioration in parents' abilities to co-operate. The Court of Appeal emphasised it is "*important for the court, in every case where fact-finding is being considered, to take time to identify the welfare issues, to understand the nature of the allegations, and then to consider whether the facts alleged are relevant to those issues and whether it is, therefore, necessary for the factual dispute to be determined.*"[118] The Court of Appeal concluded as follows:

> *"63. [...] In Re H-N, the court explained the importance of focusing on whether or not there has been coercive and controlling behaviour, as opposed to specific factual allegations of abuse. This case was decided before Re H-N, but nonetheless provides a clear example of the need identified in that case for the court (a) to focus on the overarching issue of coercive and controlling behaviour when it is raised, and (b) to do so in this context only to the extent that is relevant and necessary to determine issues as to a child's future welfare.*
>
> *64. The judge in this case did not at any stage, either in the FHDRA or fact-finding, identify the issues that arose as to the future arrangements for these three children. The judge concluded that a fact-finding hearing was required before the mother had identified the*

[117] [2022] EWCA Civ 468

[118] Ibid. para. 42

allegations she wished to pursue, and before disclosure of relevant material had been obtained.

65. A fact-finding hearing is not free-standing litigation. It always takes place within proceedings to protect a child from abuse or regarding the child's future welfare. It is not to be allowed to become an opportunity for the parties to air their grievances. Nor is it a chance for parents to seek the court's validation of their perception of what went wrong in their relationship. If fact-finding is to be justified in the first place or continued thereafter, the court must be able to identify how any alleged abusive behaviour is, or may be, relevant to the determination of the issues between the parties as to the future arrangements for the children.

66. At the risk of repeating what has been said at [37] in Re H-N and at [41] above, the main things that the court should consider in deciding whether to order a fact-finding hearing are: (a) the nature of the allegations and the extent to which those allegations are likely to be relevant to the making of the child arrangements order, (b) that the purpose of fact-finding is to allow assessment of the risk to the child and the impact of any abuse on the child, (c) whether fact-finding is necessary or whether other evidence suffices, and (d) whether fact-finding is proportionate.

67. It seems that a misunderstanding of the court's role has developed. There is a perception that the Court of Appeal has somehow made it a requirement that in every case, in which allegations of domestic abuse are made, it is incumbent upon the court to undertake fact-finding, involving a detailed analysis of each specific allegation made. That is not the case. As Re H-N explained and we reiterate here, the duty on the court is limited to determining only those factual matters which are likely to be relevant to deciding whether to make a child arrangements order and, if so, in what terms.

68. In Re H-N at [50]-[59], the court explained the correct approach where an allegation of coercive or controlling behaviour is made. The message in those paragraphs was plain. Where coercive or controlling behaviour is alleged in this context, it is likely to be the primary matter requiring determination, provided that it is likely to be relevant to a live issue relating to a child's welfare. Re H-N at [56] made clear that the focus on coercive or controlling behaviour as the primary issue should make it generally unnecessary to determine other subsidiary date-specific factual allegations.

69. Re H-N at [53] included the following sentence which may inadvertently have been misunderstood. It read:

> *Where however an issue properly arises as to whether there has been a pattern of coercive and/or controlling abusive behaviour within a family, and the determination of that issue is likely to be relevant to the assessment of the risk of future harm, a judge who fails expressly to consider the issue may be held on appeal to have fallen into error.*

70. That sentence is a requirement to consider an overarching issue of coercive or controlling behaviour, where to do so is necessary for the determination of a dispute relating to a child's welfare. It is not a requirement for the court to determine every single subsidiary factual allegation that may also be raised. The court only decides individual factual allegations where it is strictly necessary to do so in addition to determining the wider issue of coercive or controlling behaviour when that itself is necessary."

<u>Cafcass or Cafcass Cymru</u>

The initial safeguarding enquiries undertaken by Cafcass or Cafcass Cymru prior to the FHDRA stage of proceedings may provide a strong indication of the issues in the case, in particular whether there are allegations of domestic abuse and/or parental alienation. The safeguarding enquiries may in turn provide a recommendation on the necessity of a fact-finding process being undertaken.

There has been some debate in recent years however around how the Cafcass 'safeguarding' system works, and whether it should be re-modelled. In *Re H-N*, permission was given for Cafcass to intervene in proceedings, and the following submissions were made as to its role in assisting the court in deciding in cases of alleged domestic violence whether to hold a fact-finding hearing:

"38. In its submissions, Cafcass offered additional support to the court when deciding whether to hold a fact-finding hearing:

> *'It would benefit the court and the parties for there to be Cafcass involvement prior to determination of whether or not a fact-finding hearing is necessary. At present, the 'safeguarding' system and the preparation of a Cafcass 'Letter to the Court' allows a Cafcass Officer to report on allegations that have been made, but nothing more. In some cases, the allegations may be such as to make it obvious that a fact- finding hearing is required before any further assessment can take place. In others, early social work assessment could lead to a conclusion that a fact-finding hearing is not necessary, but that some other intervention would be more helpful. At present, it is rare for there to be any substantive Cafcass involvement prior to fact- finding.'*

39. In putting forward this submission, Cafcass contended that the present system was 'sub-optimal' and that, rather than a gatekeeping judge simply allocating a case for a fact-finding hearing without any social work input other than the Cafcass 'safeguarding' letter, the judge should direct that Cafcass undertake an enhanced form of safeguarding assessment (including where appropriate meeting the child) prior to the case being listed for a second gatekeeping appointment, with any resulting listing decision being made on a more informed and child-centred basis.

40. As is the case with some other submissions and suggestions that were made to the court, this offer by Cafcass (which was expressly supported by the Association of Lawyers for Children) seems to us to justify close consideration by those who are charged with reviewing PD12J."

The question which follows is: would the same be true of cases involving alleged parental alienation? Could an initial enquiry by Cafcass work for cases of alleged parental alienation to separate those where a fact-finding hearing is necessary and those where there is no need for one? Presumably, this would depend on how able an FCA is to assess the dynamic in an individual case prior to any fact-finding having taken place.

As outlined in **Chapter 1: Defining parental alienation**, Cafcass now has its own assessment tool, the CIAF,[119] for the purposes of evaluating what forces are at play for children where there are applications for a child arrangements order. The CIAF includes assessment resources for considering what may lie behind a child's refusal to spend time with their parent and/or a parent's reluctance to agree to the other parent spending time with their child. Cafcass states that the CIAF "*sets out how children may experience parental separation and how this can be understood and assessed at Cafcass,*" starting with an open question "*what is happening for this child?*" There are a number of evaluative models which seek to explore and differentiate between where there are indicators of domestic abuse, such as coercive control; where there are indicators of conflict which is harmful to the child, and where there are indicators of other forms of parenting where these are assessed as harmful to the child. All of these may give legitimate reasons for refusal/ resistance to spending time with a parent. There is also an evaluative model which indicates alternative reasons for a child's refusal/ resistance to spending time with a parent, such as alienation.

Within the tools and guidance related to alternative reasons for a child's refusal or resistance to spending time with a parent there are four different resources for evaluating what is going on for the child. One of them, the 'Alienating Behaviours Thinking Tool'[120], is directed at understanding the child's perspective and perceptions, and looking at the behaviours from both the parent and child which may indicate alienation (explored in detail in **Chapter 1: Defining parental alienation**). The tension in respect of using this framework is outlined in the notes accompanying this tool:

> "*[...] this tool should not be used in cases where the child is resisting or refusing time with a parent as a justifiable rejection e.g. when there has been domestic abuse or other forms of harmful parenting. It is also not a relevant tool when any of the other reasons for the child's*

[119] https://www.cafcass.gov.uk/grown-ups/professionals/ciaf/

[120] Available at: https://www.cafcass.gov.uk/grown-ups/professionals/ciaf/resources-for-assessing-child-refusal-resistance/

resistance or refusal e.g. affinity, attachment or the child's own independent preference are the primary factors."[121]

This is similarly reflected in the CIAF Domestic Abuse Practice Guidance which makes clear to FCAs that they must:

> *"Ensure you have clearly distinguished between harmful conflict, domestic abuse and bond breaking or alienating behaviours which lead to resistance to contact.*
>
> *Counter-allegations of alienating behaviours: perpetrators of domestic abuse will sometimes attempt to deflect blame, or reverse culpability, by making allegations that the victim is alienating the child against them. In these circumstances it is important that we are guided by the evidence/ findings and do not lose sight of the distinction between the child's 'justified', or 'appropriate rejection' of a parent (as will sometimes be the case where the child has suffered domestic abuse) and rejection caused by deliberately alienating, or unjustified behaviours."*[122]

The difficulties are self-evident, particularly the ability of Cafcass to determine whether the refusal of contact is justifiable and/or founded on a child's independent preference *without* the objective driving influences upon the child's attitude having been determined. This is particularly so where there are concurrent allegations of domestic abuse. There is no real solution, and it is difficult, in circumstances where allegations run counter to one another, for any real work to be done with children prior to fact-finding. This is further explored in **Chapter 6: The voice of the child**.

---

121 Cafcass, 'Alienating Behaviours Tool'

122 Cafcass, 'Behaviours – what are alienating behaviours?' (https://www.cafcass.gov.uk/grown-ups/parents-and-carers/divorce-and-separation/what-to-expect-from-cafcass/alienating-behaviours/)

Interim contact

Subject to Practice Direction 12J, the court is able to make a child arrangements order at an interim stage in proceedings. This power is pursuant to section 11(3) of the 1989 Act which states the court has the power to make a section 8 order at any time during the course of the proceedings in question, even though it is not in a position to dispose finally of the proceedings.

The intention of PD12J is to ensure that where allegations of domestic violence are made, there should be consideration and (if necessary) determination of those allegations at an early stage so that there is a factual matrix on which basis to make decisions about contact between a parent and a child in the future. Where does that leave applications to establish interim arrangements for the subject child?

PD12J includes consideration of what safeguarding information must be provided to the court and what its continuing obligations are in relation to the consideration of risk.[123] It also considers the principles that must be applied to the issue of interim contact *before* the determination of relevant facts[124]:

> *"25. Where the court gives directions for a fact-finding hearing, or where disputed allegations of domestic abuse are otherwise undetermined, the court should not make an interim child arrangements order unless it is satisfied that it is in the interests of the child to do so and that the order would not expose the child or the other parent to an unmanageable risk of harm (bearing in mind in particular the definition of "victim of domestic abuse" and the impact which domestic abuse against a parent can have on the emotional well-being of the child, the safety of the other parent and the need to protect against domestic abuse).*
>
> *26. In deciding any interim child arrangements question the court should–*

---

[123] PD12J, paras. 11-13

[124] PD12J, paras. 25-27

a. take into account the matters set out in section 1(3) of the Children Act 1989 or section 1(4) of the Adoption and Children Act 2002 ('the welfare check-list'), as appropriate; and

b. give particular consideration to the likely effect on the child, and on the care given to the child by the parent who has made the allegation of domestic abuse, of any contact and any risk of harm, whether physical, emotional or psychological, which the child and that parent is likely to suffer as a consequence of making or declining to make an order.

27. Where the court is considering whether to make an order for interim contact, it should in addition consider –

a. the arrangements required to ensure, as far as possible, that any risk of harm to the child and the parent who is at any time caring for the child is minimised and that the safety of the child and the parties is secured; and in particular:

i. whether the contact should be supervised or supported, and if so, where and by whom; and

ii. the availability of appropriate facilities for that purpose;

b. if direct contact is not appropriate, whether it is in the best interests of the child to make an order for indirect contact; and

c. *whether contact will be beneficial for the child."*

While some contend that the very essence of PD12J is to determine at an early stage whether contact (in principle) is in the child's best interests, others maintain that this guidance in respect of interim contact is honoured more in the breach than the observance, citing the positive emphasis on getting contact going when it has stopped.

At the same time, there are those who propound the view that the impetus for many allegations of domestic violence is to achieve a continuation of no or limited contact for cynical reasons, that PD12J is to all intents and purposes an alienator's charter. The mere suggestion of domestic abuse and accusations of coercive control can stop any prospect of interim contact in its tracks. Given the messages being given from various sources about the lack of attention paid to the issue of domestic abuse, and the need to take allegations of abuse seriously, there are those who therefore argue that there is a risk that the alienator will conceal themselves behind the cover of unfounded allegations.

<u>Conclusions</u>

The reality is too often that domestic abuse is dealt with in isolation, and only after facts are either made out or not made out does the less tangible issue of parental motive come under scrutiny. The better course is often for the issues to be heard and determined together, permitting the court to gain a holistic understanding of the dynamics involved.

On the one hand the alleged victim of domestic abuse wants findings and adequate protection from the court; on the other hand the subject of unfounded allegations made to strategically impede contact wants vindication and for the damage done to the parent child relationship to be acknowledged and repaired. That all takes court time and time is a commodity that is in short supply. At the heart of it is the irreconcilable tension that any increase in the number of fact-finding hearings or expansion of the issues to be determined within them will inevitably add to the burdens on a court system which is already struggling with significant delays. As Judd J notes in *AA v BB*[125]:

> *"I do not underestimate the difficulty of case management in proceedings such as this, or the significant pressure on the courts in finding sufficient time to deal with these cases proportionately and fairly. As well as the passages from Re H-N which I have quoted above, at paragraph 36 the President quoted from 'The Road Ahead', guidance issued in 2020;*
>
> > *'43. If the Family Court is to have any chance of delivering on the needs of children or adults who need protection from abuse, or of their families for a timely determination of applications, there will*

125 [2021] EWHC 1822 (Fam)

> *need to be a very radical reduction in the amount of time the court affords to each hearing. Parties appearing before the court should expect the issues to be limited only to those which it is necessary to determine to dispose of the case, and for oral evidence or oral submissions to be cut down only to that which it is necessary for the court to hear'. …46. Parties will not be allowed to litigate every issue…'."*[126]

However, in cases where the allegations are serious, and if founded may have a bearing on a child's refusal/ resistance to contact, the court may be faced with little choice but to engage with the factual matrix before it can even begin to consider matters of welfare.

[126] ibid. para. 43

CHAPTER FOUR

PROCEDURALLY MANAGING CASES INVOLVING ALLEGATIONS OF PARENTAL ALIENATION

The court's approach to the procedural management of intractable cases involving allegations of alienation is fluid. Whilst this has advantages in allowing case management to be tailored to the specific needs of a case, it can present its challenges too. In particular, it is recognised that much of the guidance contained within this Chapter is likely to be considered increasingly unascertainable and somewhat idealistic in the context of an overburdened court system, and the reduction in the availability of private law Legal Aid since the introduction of the Legal Aid, Sentencing and Punishment of Offenders Act 2012 ('LASPO 2012'). Nonetheless, robust procedural management can be decisive in cases involving an intractably hostile parent where allegations of alienation have been made, and how the court responds can frequently be the difference between two vastly different outcomes for the child.

This Chapter will consider some of the guidance provided by the judiciary in a number of decisions from the last two decades. It will consider the relevant parts of two key Practice Directions in the Family Procedure Rules 2010 ('FPR 2010'): PD12B (Child Arrangements Programme) and PD12J (Child Arrangements & Contact Orders: Domestic Abuse and Harm).

In particular, consideration is given to the decision of HHJ Wildblood QC in *Re A (Children) (Parental alienation),*[127] a transfer of residence case, the facts of which are explored in detail in **Chapter 7: Transfers of residence**. Whilst not a decision by an appellate court, HHJ Wildblood QC spends much time in this judgment reflecting on a "*truly exceptional*" case that had been before the Family Court on over thirty-six occasions,

[127] [2019] 9 WLUK 445

and in which ten separate professionals had been involved. A finding that the mother had alienated the children from the father had been made, and after many attempts to establish regular contact, and a failed transfer of residence, the father had reluctantly withdrawn his application. In one of the most unsatisfactory outcomes possible in private children proceedings, the children were left in a situation the court found would cause them significant and long-term emotional harm. HHJ Wildblood QC, in reflecting upon the proceedings in this judgment, summarised some of the key lessons that could be learned from how this case had been procedurally managed, and which had contributed to the difficulties in this case.

Judicial continuity

The starting point for procedural management of cases involving allegations of parental alienation is judicial continuity. Judicial continuity in the conduct of private children proceedings from the FHDRA to the making of the final order should be the objective in all cases.[128] Although frequently easier said than done, it can have a decisive impact on how a case involving allegations of parental alienation unfolds. If at case management stage a new judge begins afresh with every interim hearing, it can be difficult for the court to have a vantage point which adequately reflects the extent of historical non-compliance with court orders and agreements, in particular for proceedings which have been going on for some time. A judge is more likely to act decisively if they are aware of the full context behind interim decisions. Further, in cases where findings have been made of alienation, it will be more effective for the judge who has heard the evidence and made the findings to have conduct of the welfare aspect of a case thereon. They are likely to have a true measure of the parents and the reason why the child arrangements are proving intractable in the present.[129]

In *V v V (Children) (Contact: Implacable Hostility)*[130] (considered below and further in **Chapter 7: Transfers of residence**), Bracewell J noted that

[128] PD12B (Child Arrangements Programme), para. 10.2

[129] See Practice Direction 12J (Child Arrangements & Contact Orders – Domestic Abuse and Harm), paras. 20 & 31

[130] [2004] EWHC 1215 (Fam)

sixteen different judges had been involved over four years of litigation. Bracewell J noted that not only was this a waste of judicial time, with each judge having to read into the case at every interim hearing, it crucially risked an inconsistency of judicial approach, leading to delay and dissatisfaction on the part of the parties.[131]

The same point was made by Munby J (as he then was) in *Re D (Intractable Contact Dispute: Publicity)*[132], a decision which followed *forty-three* hearings conducted by *sixteen* different judges. Munby J made the following points, considering in particular the judgment of Wall J (as he then was) in *Re M (Intractable Contact Dispute: Interim Care Orders)*[133]:

> *"What is needed for effective case management in private law cases? The key components are not too difficult to identify:*
>
> *i) Judicial continuity: Every private law case of any complexity must be allocated to a single or at most two judges.*
>
> *ii) Timetabling: The allocated judge must set an overall timetable for the case at the earliest practicable stage. The simpler cases should be timetabled to last weeks rather than months. Even serious and complex cases should be timetabled so that they are concluded within a period measured in months rather than years.*
>
> *iii) Strategy: Proper judicial control and judicial case management requires what Wall J referred to in Re M at para [115] as "consistency of judicial approach" within the context of a judicially set "strategy for the case". This must form what he described at para [118] as "part of a wider plan for [the] children, which … needs to be thought through."*[134]

[131] ibid., para. 8

[132] [2004] EWHC 727 (Fam)

[133] [2003] EWHC 1024 (Fam)

[134] ibid., para. 49

Munby J went on to note:

> *"Too often at present, once things start going wrong, it takes too long — too often far too long — to get in front of a judge who is in a position to take potentially decisive action. Judicial case management where the case is allocated to a single judge affords real opportunities to combat this problem, particularly if the parties are able to communicate with the judge, and the judge with the parties, by fax or e-mail."*[135]

Allocation

Further, if at all possible the matter should be allocated to a District Judge, Circuit Judge or judge at High Court level in the Family Court, as opposed to the lay justices. This is also important for continuity in decision making, which will rarely be possible if the proceedings are before the lay justices or a legal adviser.

The court must consider the issue of allocation through the *President's Guidance on Allocation and Gatekeeping for Proceedings under Part II of the Children Act 1989 (Private Law)* ('Allocation Guidance'), issued in accordance with the Family Court (Composition and Distribution of Business) Rules 2014. The judiciary, including lay justices and legal advisers, have an ongoing duty to keep allocation decisions under review during proceedings,[136] in particular if issues have developed from the point of initial allocation.[137] As at the gatekeeping stage, the court will consider the appropriate level of judiciary in determining issues of allocation. Consideration will need to be given in particular to:

a. The need to make the most effective and efficient use of the local judicial resources that is appropriate, given the nature and type of application;

---

[135] ibid., para. 56

[136] In particular when any response to the application is received, safeguarding checks are received and at the FHDRA, see Allocation Guidance, para. 8

[137] Allocation Guidance, para. 28

b. The need to avoid delay;

c. The need for judicial continuity;

d. The location of the parties or any child relevant to the proceedings; and

e. Complexity.[138]

Plainly, it may be possible to argue that based on the need for judicial continuity and complexity, the matter should be re-allocated in a complex intractable case. The decision to allocate should be taken as early as possible, and an application made if necessary.

Early identification

It is essential to identify parental alienation as a key issue at an early stage in proceedings.[139] This will be more challenging in some cases than others. In cases for example where there has been a child arrangements order in place that has not been complied with thereafter, and the matter is returning before the court, it may be easier within the application to identify certain behaviours the children are presenting which indicate the respondent is influencing them, or to outline the instances of non-compliance. In a case where there has been a more recent breakdown in relations between a parent and a child, and alienation is a theme which emerges during proceedings, this may not be possible.

Avoiding delay

Section 1(2) of the 1989 Act states that: "*In any proceedings in which any question with respect to the upbringing of a child arises, the court shall have regard to the general principle that any delay in determining the question is likely to prejudice the welfare of the child.*"

---

[138] Allocation Guidance, para. 7. Considerations in respect of complexity should be made by reference to the schedule to the Allocation Guidance, see also paras. 23, 25-27

[139] *Re A (Children) (Parental Alienation)* [2019] 9 WLUK 445, para. 13(i)

In cases involving parental alienation the importance of the above statutory provision is all the more acute. Delay frequently exacerbates the difficulties, maintaining a status quo where the child is subjected to alienation in the immediate, and may ultimately lead to a situation which is irretrievable in the long-term.

In *Re D (Intractable Contact Dispute: Publicity),* considered above, a decision which came after forty-three hearings before sixteen different judges over five years, and in which Munby J (as he then was) noted the vast amount of evidence from the parties and experts that had been filed over this period (950 pages worth), the court described delays as "*the scourge of the family justice system*" and noted that in this case they were "*scandalous*", it being "a*lmost impossible to see how such a timetable can ever be compatible with the requirements of the [European] Convention [on Human Rights].*"[140] In particular, Munby J considered the frequent adjournments in the case, the delay in the court making findings in relation to the mother's various groundless or exaggerated allegations, and the delay in appointing a children's guardian all to have been detrimental to the procedural management of the case. Munby J further considered that the delay in seeking assistance from any expert other than the Cafcass officer meant the consultant clinical psychologist's "*very valuable report*" was not produced until later in proceedings, and an independent social worker was not drafted in, with the remit of facilitating and implementing overnight contact, until after the final hearing had taken place, well over two-years after contact arrangements had run into difficulties, and sixteen-months after a suspended committal order had been made. Overall Munby J concluded the following to be the three particularly concerning features in this case:

> "*i) the appalling delays of the court system, exacerbated by the absence of any meaningful judicial continuity, seemingly endless directions hearings, the lack of any overall timetable, and the failure of the court to adhere to such timetable as has been set;*

[140] *Re D (Intractable Contact Dispute: Publicity)* [2004] EWHC 727 (Fam), paras. 45-46

ii) the court's failure to get to grips with the mother's (groundless) allegations; and

iii) the court's failure to get to grips with the mother's defiance of its orders, the court's failure to enforce its own orders."[141]

In the context of *Re A (Children) (Parental alienation)*, HHJ Wildblood QC noted the impact of delay, and that the court should be cautious before repeatedly adjourning for short review hearings:

> *"At the early stage of the private law proceedings the case was adjourned repeatedly for further short reviews. I have counted that there were eight orders for review hearings in the first two years of the private law proceedings alone. That occurred, of course, before the current Children Arrangements Programme (PD 12B of The Family Procedure Rules 2010) came into force on 22nd April 2014. Paragraph 15.3 of that Programme now states: 'While it is acknowledged that an interim order may be appropriate at an early stage of court proceedings, cases should not be adjourned for a review (or reviews) of contact or other orders / arrangements and/or for addendum section 7 reports, unless such a hearing is necessary and for a clear purpose that is consistent with the timetable for the child and in the child's best interests.' Therefore, I think it very unlikely that there would a succession of review hearings like this now; this is an example of just how necessary the changes made by the Programme in this respect were."*[142]

Regrettably, delay is still, and arguably to a greater degree than when Munby J decided *Re D (Intractable Contact Dispute: Publicity)*, an inevitability in many private law cases. Nonetheless, robust and focused case management is necessary in order to ensure as little delay as possible in achieving a final order.

This does not mean that it is inappropriate to make a final order in circumstances where there is no contact between the child and non-resident parent, and evidence that such an order may not be complied

---

[141] ibid., para. 22

[142] *Re A (Children) (Parental Alienation)* [2019] 9 WLUK 445, para. 13(iii)

with. The court is constantly undertaking a balancing exercise in respect of the disadvantages of the litigation continuing as against the potential impact on the child if proceedings are resolved prematurely. When delay becomes integral in a parental alienation case is when the non-resident parent has been given repeated opportunities to comply with interim child arrangements orders, and failed to do so. Decisive action is likely to be necessary to ensure the status quo does not continue so as to keep the child within the non-resident parent's care if such circumstances will be likely to further subject them to emotional harm in the form of continuing alienation.

A full hearing of the evidence to determine allegations of fact

The safeguarding checks undertaken by Cafcass at the commencement of proceedings are likely to comment upon whether a fact-finding hearing is needed to determine allegations which are not accepted, and whether their resolution is likely to affect the court's decision. While a fact-finding hearing will not be necessary in every case, the need for some sort of determination in respect of the factual matrix underpinning the family dynamic as soon as possible is clear. It must take place as early as possible.

This issue is explored in detail in **Chapter 3: Parental alienation and domestic abuse.**

Expert assessments

The court may also consider whether it would be assisted by any social work, psychiatric, psychological or other assessment of any party or subject child to proceedings. If such a direction is sought by any party, section 13 of the CFA 2014 and Part 25 of the FPR 2010 must be complied with.

In *Re A and B (Parental Alienation: No. 1)*[143] for example, the court relied upon the evidence of a number of experts. Dr Julet Butler (psychiatrist) provided a report, followed by Dr Janine Braier (psychologist) and Ms Karen Woodall (psychotherapist). Such evidence was decisive in

---

143 [2020] EWHC 3366 (Fam)

providing an insight into the children's presentation, mental health and emotional development and behaviours, including how these differed between the children. In addition, these experts were able to comment upon the potential consequences for the children in the long-term if the status quo were to continue, and provide an insight into the family dynamics generally and the alienating parent's motivation to change. Finally, these experts were crucial in providing recommendations to the court in respect of how to progress the children's relationship with their father.

In *Re A (A Child)*[144], the Court of Appeal considered that the Recorder at first instance had been entitled to transfer residence in circumstances where this had been the firm recommendation of a psychologist, Dr Anderson, and independent social worker. The expert psychological assessment of the mother was particularly compelling; it concluded she had serious personality disorders, had a complete lack of insight into her behaviour and was unable to control her emotions towards the father. The expert psychologist concluded she was not capable of changing her behaviour, and the child's residence should indeed be changed given the parental alienation, emotional pressure and likely future psychological difficulties. The independent social worker agreed, noting that, although the child expressed a wish to stay with the mother, and the head teacher indicated a change of residence would be traumatic, continued exposure to the mother's behaviour might have an adverse effect on his emotional development.

Similarly, in *Re T (Parental Alienation)*[145] HHJ Raeside QC had evidence from Dr Tizard (chartered consultant psychologist) and Dr Shbero (clinical psychologist) in addition to the social worker and child's guardian. This evidence was decisive to the findings made by the judge, including that the child had suffered and continued to suffer emotional harm from living with her mother, denying her a positive paternal relationship, and that the mother has provided the child with a negative picture of the father which she now acts out in play. Dr Shbero provided evidence in respect of how 'torn' the child was between her parents. She

144 [2007] EWCA Civ 899

145 [2019] EWHC 3854 (Fam)

had observed, and was supported by the social worker in this regard, that in play the child had talked about wanting to destroy or crush the father, and acted aggressively towards the 'doll daddy,' wanting to stamp on him and showing the child and mummy doll standing on his face. Dr Shbero concluded that the child's behaviour and anxieties were a result of her attachment to her mother and her mother's difficulties supporting contact with the father (the mother likened the child seeing the father to an adoptive child seeing their birth family).

Perhaps most strikingly, Dr Shbero discussed the long-term consequences for the child – achieving inconsistent empathy from her mother had impacted the child's attachments, and could have had an impact on her ability to form relationships and mental health in the long-term. The lack of permission she had received to have a meaningful relationship with her father impacted her identity and well-being. Dr Shbero also concluded the mother had limited capacity to change and long-term therapy was needed to address her issues. The social worker and child's guardian supported this assessment, noting that despite therapy the mother had not shown any change in approach so far. The social worker, child's guardian and Dr Shbero's evidence weighed up the impact of different child arrangements upon the child, concluding a transfer of residence into the father's care was the appropriate solution in this case. This approach was endorsed by the judge.

All of the above decisions are considered further in **Chapter 7: Transfers of residence**, along with numerous other examples of how professional expert evidence impacted the court's findings and approach.

The court may also give permission for expert involvement, particularly independent social workers, not simply to inform its approach but to assist with matters 'on-the-ground,' including contact and handovers. As noted by Munby J (as he then was) in *Re D (Intractable Contact Dispute: Publicity)*[146]:

> *"We need to get away from the idea that experts are there simply to provide the court with reports. Directing reports can all too often turn into a source of further delay. "Is your expert really necessary?" is a*

[146] [2004] EWHC 727 (Fam)

slogan that has its uses. In this kind of case experts and other outside agencies can often be much more use helping to facilitate contact rather than writing reports — preparing mother and child for contact, actually being there at hand on Saturday morning to make sure that hand-over takes place, or even acting as the go-between if mother cannot bring herself to meet father and there is no independent friend or relative who can help."[147]

There are a number of general points to note from HHJ Wildblood's judgment in *Re A (Children) (Parental alienation)* in respect of professional and expert assistance:

i. The court should be mindful of the number of professionals involved in a case. HHJ Wildblood QC noted:

> *"These proceedings have seen a vast number of professionals. I have counted 10 and I am sure that I have omitted some. The difficulty that that creates is obvious. Each new person brings a new, personal and different insight into a case of this nature. Family members (especially children) are embarrassed about speaking of personal issues with strangers, develop litigation fatigue and learn to resent the intrusions into their lives by a succession of professional people. As the children have done, people reach a stage where they say: 'no more.'"*[148]

ii. The court should also be aware of the difficulties that can present if there is an absence of collaborative working by professionals.[149] As the following Chapters will demonstrate, there is frequently a divergence in expert opinion on the manner to resolve a case in-line with the subject child's welfare interests. However, professionals need to be united on the course that the court ultimately determines is the one that is to be adopted in order to progress matters.

[147] ibid., para. 53

[148] *Re A (Children) (Parental alienation)* [2019] 9 WLUK 445, ibid., para. 13(vi)

[149] ibid., para. 13(vii)

iii. It is important that the court has an assessment available to it which provides insight to the issues, and the way that it may resolve them. Early intervention is essential in determining what is going on, and an application should be made as early on in proceedings as possible for an expert's opinion if it is deemed necessary to assist the court in resolving the proceedings justly. As HHJ Wildblood QC noted:

> *"Early intervention is essential in a case such as this, in my opinion. It did not occur in this case. It took years (probably five) to identify the extent of the emotional and psychological issues of the mother. By that stage it was too late for there to be any effective psychotherapeutic or other intervention in relation to her, the children's views having already become so entrenched."*[150]

Regulation and qualification of experts

It also remains important that the right, qualified expert is identified, with appropriate and up-to-date experience in intractable cases. In any letter of instruction it should be made clear that parental alienation or disputed allegations of parental alienation are in issue in the case. If an expert's experience in such cases is unclear from their CV, a request for further information should be made before they are formally instructed. Further, an expert must receive all relevant documents, in particular in cases where parental alienation is an issue, and proper historical context will be relevant and may be decisive.

The consequences of this advice not being followed were explored by DJ Bailey in the decision of *B & C (Children: Child Arrangements Order)*.[151] Numerous criticisms were advanced of Ms X (child psychologist) and her conclusions by the father and paternal grandfather. In cross-examination, "*Ms X conceded that she had not done any specific training regarding parental alienation. She said that she had probably done "the odd course here and there" and that she keeps up-to-date with literature, research and books and journals she was familiar with Dr Gardner's theories regarding*

[150] ibid. para. (viii)

[151] [2018] EWFC B100

alienation."[152] DJ Bailey goes on to explain that Dr Gardener's work on parental alienation 'syndrome' has subsequently been discredited. DJ Bailey noted in his judgment that:

> *"It was put to Ms X that she had not properly examined whether this was a case which involved parental alienation. Ms X's evidence was that this was not mentioned in the letter of instruction to her. This is of some concern to this Court, as it must have been clear from the face of the papers – not least from the very first order in this case made by the lay justices on 12 July 2017 – that it was that one of the key issues in this case.* [...] "[153]

There were also other concerns regarding failures to organise her visits in a neutral location with the alienating parent (the mother) present, Ms X turning up two-hours late for her meeting with the children, observing direct contact with the paternal grandfather for just twenty minutes due to running late, and her inclusion of factually incorrect information in the report. The court ultimately concluded that limited weight could be attached to Ms X's evidence, in particular as she had received only a limited bundle and, as a result, could not consider the present circumstances in their proper historical context.

Indeed, the use of unregulated experts in proceedings involving allegations of parental alienation has gained increased media attention in recent years.[154] In December 2021 concerns were raised by the Association of Clinical Psychologists UK over the fact that psychologists who are not registered with the Health and Care Professionals Council are able to be appointed by the courts to provide expert evidence in cases.[155]

---

[152] ibid., para. 18

[153] ibid., para. 19

[154] Hannah Summers and Beatrix Campbell, The Guardian, 'Parental alienation and the unregulated experts shattering children's lives', 12 June 2022, (https://www.theguardian.com/global-development/2022/jun/12/parental-alienation-and-the-unregulated-experts-shattering-childrens-lives)

[155] Association of Clinical Psychologists UK, 'The Protection of the Public in the Family Courts', December 2021 (https://acpuk.org.uk/the-protection-of-the-public-in-the-family-courts/)

As noted by Sir Andrew McFarlane PFD: "*Where the issue of parental alienation is raised and it is suggested that an expert should be instructed, the court must be careful only to authorise such instruction where the individual expert has relevant expertise.*"[156] In particular, attention is drawn to the 'President's Memorandum: Experts in the Family Court',[157] where Sir Andrew McFarlane PFD emphasises that an "*expert must demonstrate to the court that he or she has the relevant knowledge and experience to give their opinion evidence, or factual evidence which is not based exclusively on personal observation or sensation*", and says that an expert must be impartial and that "*the court will refuse to authorise or admit the evidence of an expert whose methodology is not based on any established body of knowledge.*" Sir Andrew McFarlane PFD concludes by saying:

> "*The Family Court adopts a rigorous approach to the admission of expert evidence. As the references in this memorandum make plain, pseudo-science, which is not based on any established body of knowledge, will be inadmissible in the Family Court.*"

[156] Sir Andrew McFarlane, 'Speech by the President of the Family Division: Supporting Families in Conflict – There is a better way', Jersey International Family Law Conference 2021, page 13 (https://www.judiciary.uk/announcements/speech-by-the-president-of-the-family-division-supporting-families-in-conflict-there-is-a-better-way/)

[157] Sir Andrew McFarlane, 'President's Memorandum: Experts in the Family Court', 4 October 2021 (https://www.judiciary.uk/wp-content/uploads/2021/10/PFD-Memo-Experts.pdf)

The Family Justice Council has recently published interim guidance[158] regarding expert witnesses in cases where allegations of alienating behaviours are made. It emphasises the importance of ensuring that the instructed expert has a reliable body of knowledge or experience to underpin their evidence. It points to the Family Justice Council/ British Psychological Society's guidance for psychologists as expert witnesses in family proceedings,[159] and also emphasises the importance of the court being alert to possible conflicts of interest, in particular where the expert recommends an intervention or therapy that they or an associate would benefit financially from delivering. The Family Justice Council's interim guidance concludes that conflicts of interest can be avoided by letters of instruction being carefully considered to identify the issues and preserve the independence and integrity of the assessment. This may include, for example, clarifying in any letter of instruction that there should be no variation of the terms of the instructions between the assessor and any party without the revisions being considered by the court at a hearing on notice to all. Further, the interim guidance recommends close scrutiny of any further recommended work. The court should actively consider, before further work is ordered with the appointed expert who has assessed within the proceedings or someone with a related financial interest, whether the court should endorse this approach and whether it has scrutinised all available options.

Section 7 reports

The court will frequently consider, at the appropriate juncture, directing that a report is prepared under section 7 of the 1989 Act in respect of specified matters relating to the welfare of the subject child. In particular,

---

158 Family Justice Council, 'Interim Guidance in relation to expert witnesses in cases where there are allegations of alienating behaviours – conflicts of interest', May 2022 (https://www.judiciary.uk/wp-content/uploads/2022/05/FJC-interim-Guidance-use-of-experts-in-cases-with-allegations-of-alienating-behaviours.pdf). It is anticipated the full guidance will be issued in 2023.

159 The British Psychological Society, 'Psychologists as Expert Witnesses in the family courts in England and Wales: Standards, competencies and expectations', May 2022 (https://www.bps.org.uk/sites/www.bps.org.uk/files/Policy/Policy%20-%20Files/Psychologists%20as%20Expert%20Witness%20in%20family%20courts%20in%20England%20and%20Wales%20-%20standards%2C%20competencies%20and%20expectations.pdf)

in cases in which it appears that a child is at risk of being a victim of domestic abuse, or there is a risk of harm to a child resulting from domestic abuse, the court should consider, unless not necessary to safeguard the subject child's interests, directing a report on the question of contact, or any other matters relating to the welfare of any subject child of proceedings.[160]

A section 7 report shall be prepared either by:

i. a Cafcass / Cafcass Cymru officer or FCA;

ii. the local authority, in circumstances where the court determines this is preferable based on the information that has been provided about the extent and nature of the local authority's current or recent involvement with the subject of the application and the parties[161]; or

iii. an independent social worker. If such a direction is sought, section 13 of the CFA 2014 and Part 25 of the FPR 2010 must be complied with.

The report can be in writing or orally, however is most commonly the former.

It should be noted that a fact-finding hearing should generally occur before a report under section 7 of the 1989 Act is ordered. This is reflected in cases involving allegations of domestic abuse by the express requirement under PD12J that if the court directs there should be a fact-finding hearing on the issue of domestic abuse, the court will not usually request a section 7 report until *after* that hearing, and in that event the court should direct that any judgment is provided to Cafcass, or alternatively an agreed list of findings.[162]

Regardless, if a section 7 report has been filed prior to fact-finding, at the conclusion of any fact-finding hearing the court must consider,

---

160 Practice Direction 12J, para. 21

161 Practice Direction 12B, para. 14.13

162 Practice Direction 12J, para. 22

notwithstanding any earlier report, whether the child's interests necessitates further directions about the preparation or scope of any report under section 7. Proceedings may be adjourned for the officer to make representations about the preparation or scope of further enquiries.[163]

The report will be on such matters relating to the welfare of the children who are subject to proceedings. If ordered, the court should direct which specific matters relating to the welfare of the child are to be addressed. They will generally only be ordered in cases where there is a dispute as to with whom the child should live, spend time, or otherwise have contact with, and can also be ordered if there is an issue concerning the child's wishes, alleged risk to the child, or where information and advice is needed which the court considers necessary before a decision can be reached.[164] The court should state on the face of the order the specific factual and/or other issue which is to be addressed in the focused report.[165]

When preparing a section 7 report, the author is encouraged to make recommendations for the stepped phasing-in of child arrangements (i.e. recommendations for the medium and longer term future for the child) insofar as they are able to do so safely in the interests of the child concerned.[166]

Pursuant to paragraph 30 of PD12J a section 7 report post-fact-finding should however address the factors set out in paragraphs 36 and 37, unless the court directs otherwise:

> *36. (1) In the light of:*
>
> > *(a) any findings of fact,*
> >
> > *(b) admissions; or*

---

[163] Practice Direction 12J, para. 30

[164] Practice Direction 12B, para. 14.13

[165] ibid.

[166] Practice Direction 12B, para. 15.4

(c) domestic abuse having otherwise been established,

the court should apply the individual matters in the welfare checklist with reference to the domestic abuse which has occurred and any expert risk assessment obtained.

(2) In particular, the court should in every case consider any harm-

(a) which the child as a victim of domestic abuse, and the parent with whom the child is living, has suffered as a consequence of that domestic abuse; and

(b) which the child and the parent with whom the child is living is at risk of suffering, if a child arrangements order is made.

(3) The court should make an order for contact only if it is satisfied-

(a) that the physical and emotional safety of the child and the parent with whom the child is living can, as far as possible, be secured before, during and after contact; and

(b) that the parent with whom the child is living will not be subjected to further domestic abuse by the other parent.

37. In every case where a finding or admission of domestic abuse is made, or where domestic abuse is otherwise established, the court should consider the conduct of both parents towards each other and towards the child and the impact of the same. In particular, the court should consider –

(a) the effect of the domestic abuse on the child and on the arrangements for where the child is living;

(b) the effect of the domestic abuse on the child and its effect on the child's relationship with the parents;

(c) whether the parent is motivated by a desire to promote the best interests of the child or is using the process to continue a form of domestic abuse against the other parent;

(d) the likely behaviour during contact of the parent against whom findings are made and its effect on the child; and

(e) the capacity of the parents to appreciate the effect of past domestic abuse and the potential for future domestic abuse.

Conclusions

In *V v V (Children) (Contact: Implacable Hostility),* considered above and decided as long ago as 2004, Bracewell J makes the following comment:

> *"2. [...] Constant litigation in respect of residence and/or contact is not only destabilising for parents and children who become a battleground to be fought over at any cost, but it is a process which progressively results in entrenched attitudes as if engaged in a war of attrition. [...]*
>
> *3. In this case there has been constant litigation since the year 2000, which has involved 17 court orders and directions and 16 different judges, including a full hearing before Bodey J. in 2002 in the High Court, and still the case drags on. [...]*
>
> *7. It appears to me that there are ways in which the problems can be addressed. The first consists of improvements in the court process. These are limited and mainly procedural, and will certainly require additional resources. They consist of case management from the date of application to the court, judicial continuity, timetabling to suit the needs of the case and not the slots made available by court listing, proactive orders such as envisaged by Munby J. in Re D , and attaching conditions to residence orders under s.11(7) Children Act 1989. Such improvements are dependent upon a change in the role of CAFCASS officers, so that in addition to writing reports, which must be timetabled to the needs of the case, as opposed to waiting for the availability of an officer to undertake the task, the officer will be there to monitor the initial stages of contact, help with hand-over arrangements and, if necessary, bring the case back to court before the same judge if problems arise. Such monitoring at an early stage has real potential to prevent frustration and animosity between parents. It*

> *needs to be combined with well resourced, supervised and specialist contact centres, of which there are currently too few.*
>
> *8. Some parents agree to contact without any intention of making it work, as I find in the current case. At present it can take months for a case to be restored to court when contact has been frustrated. Further delays then occur in a search for a solution, during which time there may be no contact taking place and the residential parent, usually the mother, uses the time to brainwash the child into rejection of the father. The father then applies to commit the mother to prison, by which time there is no hope of an outcome which meets the need of the child to have a good relationship with both parents. The effect of intervention by a CAFCASS officer at the earliest stage would enable these cases to be brought back to court, overnight if necessary, before the same judge. Such improvements in procedure are supported by all the judges, but are frustrated by the lack of resources to deliver. Judicial continuity is essential. For a succession of judges to have to read a case for the first time, often consisting of many bundles, is not only wasteful of judicial time, but it risks inconsistency of approach and adds to delay and dissatisfaction of the parties.*
>
> *9. There are undoubtedly difficulties in achieving continuity, particularly in the county courts and the family proceeding courts. In the former jurisdiction full-time judges have other duties in criminal and civil courts which may remove them from family work for months at a time; and part-time recorders, by definition, sit for limited periods in the year. In the family proceedings courts it is by no means easy to convene the same bench of magistrates at short notice. However, these problems are capable of solution and must be addressed by the Court Service."*

Sadly, Bracewell J's summations of the problems caused by delay, lack of judicial continuity, and lack of effective intervention and monitoring from Cafcass at the earliest stages of proceedings are perhaps more true now than they were in 2004. Resource concerns have only worsened and, as the court systems continue to be burdened by challenges, cases involving implacable hostility have become yet more difficult to procedurally manage. It is in this context that it is more important than ever to effectively and robustly case manage proceedings, and to be alive to the different options available to the court that may assist in unlocking an intractable case.

CHAPTER FIVE

OPTIONS AVAILABLE FOR THE COURT

There are a wide spectrum of options available for the court in remedying situations of parental alienation. The manner in which the court responds will be dependent upon the severity of the situation. At one end of the spectrum are simple attempts at reasoning with a parent; at the other is a change in the child's main home, or a transfer of residence (explored further in **Chapter 7: Transfers of residence**).

It was recently acknowledged by Peter Jackson LJ in *Re S (Parental Alienation: Cult)*[167] that "*[c]ases at the upper end of the spectrum of alienation place exceptional demands on the court [...] [and] the more distant the relationship with the unfavoured parent becomes, the more limited its powers become [...].*"[168] Nonetheless, the court has a duty to act as necessary, and if the court does not attempt to remedy the intractable situation which presents itself, it risks breaching its procedural obligations under Article 8 of the ECHR (as explored in **Chapter 2: General principles regarding contact**). Peter Jackson LJ goes on to note:

> "*In summary, in a situation of parental alienation the obligation on the court is to respond with exceptional diligence and take whatever effective measures are available. The situation calls for judicial resolve because the line of least resistance is likely to be less stressful for the child and for the court in the short term. But it does not represent a solution to the problem. Inaction will probably reinforce the position of the stronger party at the expense of the weaker party and the bar will be raised for the next attempt at intervention. Above all, the obligation on the court is to keep the child's medium to long term welfare at the forefront of its mind and wherever possible to uphold the child and parent's right to respect for family life before it is breached. In making*

167 [2020] EWCA Civ 568

168 ibid., para. 11

its overall welfare decision the court must therefore be alert to early signs of alienation. What will amount to effective action will be a matter of judgment, but it is emphatically not necessary to wait for serious, worse still irreparable, harm to be done before appropriate action is taken. It is easier to conclude that decisive action was needed after it has become too late to take it."[169]

The court will at all times aim to resolve the intractable situation in a manner which negatively impacts the child to the least possible extent. Nonetheless, a theme that will emerge in this Chapter (as in **Chapter 7: Transfers of residence**) is just how varied the approaches to managing these cases are. Expert opinion will frequently differ as to the most appropriate course of action; the court will often be presented with divergent views held, not just by the parties but by the professionals too, as to how to unlock an intractable case.

This Chapter considers some possible options that are available for the court.

Persuasion

The most obvious method adopted by the court is to simply reason with the relevant parent and persuade them to take the right course of action for the benefit of the children involved.

Unsurprisingly, this is the approach in cases involving alienation that will often have the least success. A parent's intractability will frequently be the reason the matter is before the Family Court, and has not been resolved by consent. However, in the right sort of case, and when the parent has the right sort of representation and advice, the impact of persuasion and imploring a parent to reason should not be underestimated. In circumstances where serious findings have been made, persuasion alone may achieve the desired result. Through highlighting some of the more robust methods that could be resorted to in the event of non-compliance, the court can be extremely persuasive:

[169] ibid., para. 13

the looming risk of a fundamental revision in the child arrangements may be all that is required to achieve a change in approach.

<u>Interim child arrangements orders</u>

The court is able under section 8 of the 1989 Act make a child arrangements order regulating arrangements relating to:

a. *With whom* a child is to live, spend time or otherwise have contact, and

b. *When* a child is to live, spend time or otherwise have contact with any person.

Subject to Practice Direction 12J (considered further in **Chapter 3: Parental alienation and domestic abuse**), the court is able to make a child arrangements order at an interim stage in proceedings. This power is pursuant to section 11(3) of the 1989 Act which states the court has the power to make a section 8 order at any time during the course of the proceedings in question, even though it is not in a position to dispose finally of the proceedings.

An interim child arrangements order has the following objectives:

i. It aims to re-instate the relationship between the parent and the non-resident parent in a manner that is controlled by the court. The court is able to make an interim determination as to the best way to re-introduce the non-resident parent to the alienated child, and can combine this with other methods such as therapeutic intervention, for example (see below). Consideration will be given as to how and when contact should be facilitated in order for it to be effective.

ii. It provides a 'testing ground' for the court to re-introduce contact with judicial and expert oversight. It is often more productive for a 'trial and error' approach to re-introducing contact to be undertaken, in particular with the benefit of a children's guardian or social worker supervising some of the contact, for example. In cases involving alienation where the court may need to engage flexibly with the case, this allows the court a window into what may need to be remedied in its approach, which can be essential in the court arriving at a solution for the family which actually works. It would be inadequate for a final order to be arrived at, and for proceedings to conclude without the court having grappled at all with the child's objections and the actual implementation of contact arrangements.

iii. In circumstances where the allegation is that one parent is not adequately promoting contact, or that the children are exhibiting behaviours that suggest alienation has occurred, it can be useful to have professionals observe and comment upon this in order for the court to make findings, or to simply inform the court's general approach.

An interim child arrangements order is a determination of a question in respect of the upbringing of a child, and therefore pursuant to section 1 of the 1989 Act the child's welfare shall be the court's paramount consideration. In considering whether to make, vary or discharge an order under section 8 of the 1989 Act in circumstances where it is opposed by any party to the proceedings (section 1(4)(a) of the 1989 Act), the court shall have regard to the 'welfare checklist' at section 3, namely:

a. The ascertainable wishes and feelings of the child concerned (considered in the light of his age and understanding)[170];

b. His physical, emotional and educational needs;

c. The likely effect on him of any change in his circumstances;

d. His age, sex, background and any characteristics of his which the court considers relevant;

e. Any harm which he has suffered or is at risk of suffering;

---

[170] See **Chapter 5: The voice of the child**

f. How capable each of his parents, and any other person in relation to whom the court considers the question to be relevant, is of meeting his needs;

g. The range of powers available to the court under this Act in the proceedings in question.

The court will be guided by all of the evidence before it, including but not limited to any reports that have been prepared by the children's guardian, Cafcass FCA or social worker. This may be a report prepared under section 7 on the welfare of the child, if the proceedings are at the stage where one has been ordered and filed.

Pursuant to section 11(7), an order under section 8 may:

a. Contain directions about how it is to be carried into effect;

b. Impose conditions which must be complied with by any person –

    i. Who is named in the order as a person with whom the child concerned is to live, spend time or otherwise have contact;

    ii. Who is parent of the child;

    iii. Who is not a parent of his but who has parental responsibility for him; or

    iv. With whom the child is living,

   and to whom the conditions are expressed to apply;

c. Be made to have effect for a specified period, or contain provisions which are to have effect for a specified period;

d. Make such incidental, supplemental or consequential provision as the court thinks fit.

In considering what, if any, sort of interim child arrangements order should be made, the court will often be tasked with deciding whether the order should be for direct contact, indirect contact or a combination of the both.

Direct contact

In deciding whether to make an order for interim direct contact, the court will first consider whether such contact should be supervised or supported in some capacity.[171] In circumstances where there are allegations of domestic abuse and potential safeguarding concerns, supervision or support may be deemed necessary to ensure that any risk of harm to the child and the parent who is at any time caring for the child is minimised, and that the safety of the child and the parties is secured.[172] This tension is explored further in **Chapter 3: Parental alienation and domestic abuse**.

However, in circumstances where there are no allegations of domestic abuse, or a fact-finding hearing has occurred and no findings have been made, there may still be advantages in supported or supervised contact taking place, in particular in circumstances where a children's guardian or social worker is involved with the family. In some circumstances, parents may choose to fund supervision by an independent social worker. Not only may professionals be able to offer their opinion to the court as outlined above, they may be able to assist in facilitating and improving the chances of success in re-establishing contact. For example, they may be able to:

i. Offer advice to the non-resident parent when faced with challenging behaviour from the children;

ii. Offer advice to the resident parent on how to communicate with the child in advance of contact, in particular on how to encourage them to attend contact; or

171 See Practice Direction 12J, para. 27(a)(i)

172 See Practice Direction 12J, paras. 25-27 for further detail on the court's various considerations when making an interim order in cases where there are allegations of domestic abuse.

iii. Help to facilitate the practicalities of the handover between the resident and non-resident parent.

Caution needs to be exercised however, and a balance achieved. On the other side of the debate it may be said that where there are no safeguarding concerns and the ultimate aim is to reassure the child, the presence of third-parties should be kept to a minimum and supervision may prove unhelpful.

In terms of where direct contact should take place, again this is a judgment call that will depend upon a number of factors. While contact at the non-resident parent's home may be the ideal, it may be useful to commence contact on more neutral territory, such as in the community.

Alternatively, contact within a contact centre may be the easiest way of ensuring supervision or support is available, in particular if supervision or support is not available through any alternative means. It does however frequently come at a cost. It can also be a restrictive and artificial environment for the child, and may make it more challenging thereafter to progress from a contact centre to the non-resident's parent's home, which has obvious limitations in circumstances where the goal in the long-term is a progression to day-contact at the non-resident parent's home or overnight contact.

Indirect contact

Indirect contact can include communication by letter or email; telephone contact (calls or texts), or video contact. It can be unregulated, or, alternatively, at specific, set times.

Indirect contact can have an appeal at the early stages of re-introducing contact. It may be that a child expresses a desire for some contact, but wishes for it to commence on an indirect basis. It also may be that the non-resident parent suggests indirect contact should take place initially in order to re-establish a relationship between the parent and the child, before progressing to direct contact at a later stage. The advantage of this sort of approach is that it is more likely to be at the child's pace, and it may improve the likelihood of a child being more amenable to a progression to direct forms of contact in due course.

On the other hand, as pointed out by HHJ Wildblood QC in *Re A (Children) (Parental alienation)*[173]:

> *"The use of indirect contact in a case where there is parental alienation has obvious limitations, as this case demonstrates. The father's letters, cards and presents were being sent to him into a home environment where he was 'demonised', to use the terminology of Dr Berelowitz. They served no purpose in maintaining any form of relationship between the father and the children. It is regrettable that there was not more perseverance in the earlier private proceedings to resolve the obstructions to contact."*[174]

The court therefore must be aware of limitations to indirect contact. In cases where a child has been alienated, and remains in an environment where alienation continues, the sending of a letter or email to a child may not guarantee anything by way of response. It relies upon the child being shown the correspondence, it (potentially) being read to them, and thereafter the child being encouraged to respond. All of these things require a degree of co-operation by the resident parent, and are difficult to monitor and regulate. It is also relatively easy for a child to disengage from indirect contact, either by refusing to answer a call, refusing to put on the video during video contact, or refusing to respond altogether. For younger children in particular, their attention span may necessarily limit the effectiveness of this sort of contact– it depends on their ability to sit still in front of a video, read and write, etc. Regardless of age, indirect contact poses challenges, in particular in circumstances where there will likely be resistance, whether due to false beliefs about the non-resident parent or by virtue of the relationship with the non-resident parent no longer existing, or ever having existed.

Whilst a useful order in appropriate cases, and something that can potentially be used alongside an order for direct contact, relying solely on indirect contact risks re-enforcing the impact of alienation by failing to address the problem head-on, and in some instances sending a signal that contact needs to be in some way managed or controlled.

---

[173] [2019] 9 WLUK 445

[174] ibid., para. 13(v)

Activity directions and conditions

Section 11A of the 1989 Act allows the court to direct that a party is to undertake an activity that would, in the court's opinion, help to establish, maintain or improve the involvement in the life of the child concerned of that individual or another party to the proceedings (section 11(3)). This is called an 'activity direction.'

Where the court is considering whether to make provision about with whom/ when the child is to live or spend time/ have contact with any person by making, varying or discharging a child arrangements order, the court may make an activity direction (section 11A(1A)-(2)). The court may also make such an order when the court is considering whether a person has failed to comply with a child arrangements order, or what steps to take in consequence of that persons' failure (section 11A(2A) & (2B)).

In considering the making of an activity direction, the welfare of the child concerned is the court's paramount consideration (section 11A(9)).

The activities that person may be required to undertake include programmes, classes and counselling or guidance sessions that may assist the parent in establishing, maintaining or improving contact with a child, or in addressing violent behaviour so as to enable them to facilitate involvement in a child's life. Alternatively, sessions can simply provide the participant with information or advice as to making or operating arrangements for the involvement in a child's life (section 11A(5)). However, an activity direction cannot be used to force anyone to undergo medical or psychiatric examination, assessment or treatment, or to take part in mediation (section 11A(6)).

In the context of parental alienation cases, the court will primarily be considering activity directions that assist the alienating parent to understand the importance of complying with any child arrangements order that has previously been made, and making contact work. This will be in addition to helping them establish, maintain or improve the involvement of the non-resident parent in the child's life.

Unlike an activity direction, an 'activity condition' under section 11C of the 1989 Act is a direction that is made when the court makes or varies a child arrangements order containing (or adding, varying or omitting) provision for a child to live with different persons at different times, and provision regulating arrangements relating to with whom or when the child is to spend time/ have contact with any person (section 11C(1)). In other words, the basic distinction is that a direction is made whilst the case is ongoing; a condition is attached to a 'final' child arrangements order. The activities that may be required by an activity condition are the same as under an activity direction (section 11C(5)).

Before making a contact activity direction or condition the court must satisfy itself about the appropriateness of what it is proposing to impose, including (section 11E(2) to (6)):

i. That the activity proposed to be specified in the order is appropriate in the circumstances of the case.

ii. That the person proposed to be specified as the provider of the activity is suitable to provide the activity.

iii. That the activity proposed to be specified is provided in a place to which the individual who would be subject to the direction or condition can reasonably be expected to travel.

iv. The likely effect of the direction or condition upon the individual who is to be subject to it, including any conflict with their religious beliefs, and any interference with the times (if any) at which they normally work or attend an educational establishment.

The court is able to ask a Cafcass officer to provide the court with information in respect of these matters (section 11E(7)).

It should also be noted that section 11G enables the court to ask the Cafcass officer to monitor and report on compliance with any activity direction that has been made, or any activity condition that has been imposed upon the making or varying of a child arrangements order. If requested, Cafcass is under a duty to provide this information to the court. This is a useful tool in ensuring that the court is informed of any failures to comply with activity directions or conditions. In addition, as the *Guidance to Cafcass and practitioners on their roles in supporting the courts in their use of the s11A-P provisions* (Cafcass Guidance on s11A-P) notes, the court may also ask Cafcass to provide information beyond compliance about the *impact*, beneficial or otherwise, of attendance, in terms of helping to address the issues in the case. Whatever Cafcass is being asked to do, there will therefore need to be liaison with the provider, and any relevant information from them should be reported to the court, together with any additional Cafcass analysis and recommendations. The Cafcass Guidance on s11A-P also notes that in some cases, the Cafcass officer will have been asked by the court to have other forms of involvement with the parties and/or the child during the period of participation in the contact activities, the outcome of which should also be reported to the court.[175]

Separated parents information programmes ('SPIPs')

The Cafcass Guidance on s11A-P refers to three types of activity that the court can direct a person to engage with under either an activity direction or condition. This includes information meetings about mediation, domestic abuse prevention programmes, and SPIPs.[176]

The SPIP is most commonly recommended by the Cafcass officer in intractable disputes. It may be recommended within the safeguarding letter to the court following safeguarding checks that have been undertaken by Cafcass upon the issue of the application, or alternatively as part of the recommendations that are in a section 7 report. The report may comment upon the attitude of the parties towards attending a SPIP.

Upon being ordered by the court, the Cafcass officer involved in the case can make a referral to a local organisation which will provide the SPIP, working in partnership with Cafcass. If the parties are referred through Cafcass, there is no charge for them to attend.

---

[175] Cafcass Guidance on s11A-P, para. 2.6

[176] Cafcass Guidance on s11A-P, para. 2.2

The SPIP will usually be delivered to mixed groups of parents in one four-hour session, or two two-hour sessions. Generally, both parties will be required to partake in a SPIP. However, they will not be expected to go to the same course. The course looks at how the parties may work as separated parents in the best interests of the children, including work around parent communication and the emotional effects of separation and the options for moving forward.[177] Their popularity in proceedings is probably due to their wide availability, and the fact they are a one-off measure that does not require excessive commitment on the part of parents. Whether this makes them less effective is another question. The court should always be conscious that the alienating parent is likely to have their preconceived ideas of the non-resident parent, especially if findings have been made of alienation. A SPIP is relatively easy to comply with, even reluctantly, and in considering the appropriateness of it, the court should evaluate whether it is going to be an effective measure in undoing months, or indeed years, of ingrained patterns of behaviour. SPIPs are likely to be part of a menu of options the court uses, as opposed to the decisive factor in unlocking an intractable case.

Improving Child and Family Arrangements ('ICFA')

ICFA is the term used to cover a range of programmes designed by Cafcass to assist in cases when it is assessed that conflict between parents is preventing contact from progressing in a meaningful way. In cases where it is considered an ICFA may be beneficial, Cafcass may make a recommendation to the court that parents should be referred to one of five regional approved providers. The next stage is for the court to make an order for the referral. Thereafter the FCA will make a referral to the requisite ICFA provider, including information about the family and their assessment of what is needed to move forward to agree safe, beneficial and sustainable child arrangements.

Generally, parents are also expected to attend a SPIP alongside the ICFA.

[177] Cafcass, Separated Parents Information Programme, (https://www.cafcass.gov.uk/grown-ups/parents-and-carers/divorce-and-separation/parenting-together/separated-parents-information-programme/)

An ICFA referral will require commitment from the parents to improve contact. The approach encourages collaboration, and allows for parents to be involved with planning how the contact should progress. Once the referral has been made the parents will be asked to complete a Proposed Work Plan (PWP), setting out the agreed work to be undertaken to achieve better arrangements for the children.

The work thereafter can take different forms, but the most common is a programme over a few weeks which is structured to reintroduce a child to a non-resident parent. Possible forms of intervention may include:

- Meeting with parents individually and/or together to help them resolve issues, prepare for time with the child, and agree a Parenting Plan.

- Working directly with the child to prepare them for time with their parent or family member.

- Observation of the time the child spends with the parent or family member, offering guidance and support where necessary, and providing further insight into any potential risks.

Programmes will generally be tailored to each individual family and their needs. The ICFA provider will generally provide a final report of the work that is to be undertaken, which will thereafter inform the Cafcass FCA's further assessment and report to the court.

Since the introduction of IFCA in May 2021 (replacing Child Contact Interventions or 'CCIs'), the use of this resource has proven popular. It can provide a useful tool in private children law cases, particularly those involving intractable disputes, by offering parties a degree of control over the procedure for agreeing arrangements, and facilitating within a structured setting the commencement of the same.

Cafcass have published a helpful guide about the use of ICFAs, and how they may help families to agree child arrangements and contact.[178]

---

178 https://www.cafcass.gov.uk/download/14308/

Monitoring of child arrangement orders

In proceedings in which the court makes or varies a child arrangements order, pursuant to section 11H the court may ask a Cafcass officer to continue to monitor compliance with a child arrangements order and report to the court on such matters relating to compliance as the court may specify (sections 11H(1) & (2)). This can be hugely effective in ensuring that there is a degree of oversight in circumstances where a parent has historically been resistant to contact, and orders have historically been breached.

The court can make this request upon making or varying the child arrangements order, or, at any time during the subsequent course of the proceedings as they relate to contact or to the child's living arrangements (section 11H(5)). Such an order can therefore relate to the period that the proceedings are before the court or alternatively, or in addition, the period after proceedings have ended.

An order cannot however exceed twelve months (section 11H(6)). The people who can be subject to monitoring are: a person who is required to allow contact with a child; a person whose contact with the child is provided for; and, a person who is subject to a condition under section 11(7)(b) (see above) (section 11H(3)).

The Cafcass Guidance on s11A-P provides detailed and useful assistance for practitioners and the court in determining whether such a requirement is necessary. In summary:

i. The general assumption is that the provision should not be used in 'consent order' cases where the proceedings have ended. Consideration of its use should be limited to cases where the issue of contact has remained in dispute during the proceedings, and where a trial and judicial determination of the child arrangements order has taken place. For example, if there is a strong feeling of dissatisfaction by one or both of the parties.[179]

[179] Cafcass Guidance, para. 3.2

ii. Consent of the parties is not required (unlike family assistance orders, see below).[180]

iii. The court may end the proceedings with a child arrangements order that has a monitoring requirement, or alternatively it can set a review hearing (usually before the same judge).[181]

iv. In both cases, timely monitoring of compliance order is necessary, and likely to take the form of telephone contact between the Cafcass officer, the parties and the children (if of sufficient age and level of understanding). The focus of the monitoring should be on the issue of whether there has been compliance with the terms of the order – it is neither a punitive or welfare intervention. If early contacts indicate that there has been requisite compliance, it may be appropriate for the Cafcass officer to reduce the frequency with which monitoring takes place (in particular if the requirement for monitoring lasts over many months).[182]

v. Non-compliance will usually involve either an absolute refusal by the resident parent to allow contact to take place (either immediately or at a later stage), or a chronic situation characterised by a series of minor failures to observe the terms of the child arrangements order.[183]

vi. The court may request to be notified in writing about the outcome of monitoring, either at the end of the period in question, or, if compliance has been inadequate, at an earlier stage. Non-compliance, in particular chronic cases of various minor failures, should not be allowed to 'drag on.' If the Cafcass officer views there has been non-compliance, they should notify the court, including details of the series of minor or more major infractions.[184]

---

[180] Cafcass Guidance, para. 3.2

[181] Cafcass Guidance, para. 3.3

[182] Cafcass Guidance, para. 3.3

[183] Cafcass Guidance, para. 3.4

[184] Cafcass Guidance, para. 3.4

vii. When the court receives such a notification from Cafcass, it may choose to bring forward the review date if one has been set. If proceedings are at an end, the court will need to await enforcement proceedings being brought.[185]

viii. The Cafcass officer should send any notification sent to the court to the parties, and will need to consider how/whether its contents should be communicated to the affected children. The Cafcass officer should continue to monitor compliance while the guidance of the court is awaited about how it will deal with the reported non-compliance.[186]

ix. The task of monitoring compliance may be undertaken by a Family Support Worker, working in consultation with the Cafcass officer who has undertaken the bulk of the work during the previous proceedings, or is undertaking work during ongoing proceedings.[187]

Such orders can be effective inducement to the resident parent to comply with the terms of a child arrangements order, with the threat of further court intervention always looming in the event of non-compliance. They also ensure there is a degree of professional oversight, whether during proceedings or thereafter. This can be evidentially useful for the court to have a better sense of what is happening 'on-the-ground.' It also means that an independent third-party can alert the court to non-compliance, and trigger further judicial oversight before matters become even more intractable.

---

[185] Cafcass Guidance, para. 3.5

[186] Cafcass Guidance, para. 3.5

[187] Cafcass Guidance, para. 3.6

Family assistance orders

Pursuant to section 16 of the 1989 Act, in any family proceedings, the court has the power to make an order requiring a Cafcass officer or an officer from the local authority[188] to advise, assist (and where appropriate) befriend any person named in the order (section 16(1)). The person can be anyone with whom the child is living or who has an order for contact with respect to the child – a parent, guardian, or special guardian of the child. It can of course be the child themselves (section 16(2)).

If the court makes a family assistance order with respect to a child and the order is to be in force at the same time as a contact provision contained in a child arrangements order regulating arrangements relating to with whom the child is to spend time/otherwise have contact, the family assistance order may direct the officer concerned to give advice and assistance as regards to establishing, improving or maintaining contact with the non-resident parent (section 16(4A)). Where the family assistance order is made alongside other types of orders under section 8 of the 1989 Act, it may direct the officer concerned report to the court on such matters relating to the section 8 order as the court may require (such as whether the order ought to be varied or discharged) (section 16(6)).

Unlike monitoring requirements under section 11H (considered above), no court can make a family assistance order unless it has obtained the consent of every person to be named in the order, other than the child (section 16(3)). Unless the court specifies a shorter period, a family assistance order shall have effect for a period of twelve months beginning with the date on which it is made (section 16(5)).

Pursuant to Practice Direction 12M, before making a family assistance order the court must have obtained the opinion of the appropriate officer regarding whether it would be in the best interests of the child for an order to be made and, if so, how the family assistance order could operate

[188] Note pursuant to section 16(7) the family assistance order shall not be made so as to require a local authority to make an officer of theirs available unless the authority agree, or, the child concerned lives or will live within their area.

and for what period.[189] This may be given orally or in writing (i.e. in a section 7 report).[190] Any persons it is proposed should be named in the order should have the opportunity to comment upon the same.[191]

Practitioners are also advised to consult the *Cafcass Family Assistance Order Guidance*[192] for further detail, including the test that is applied by Cafcass when considering commencement of a family assistance order. It is important to note that within this, there is a summary of the factors that contribute to a family assistance order working well, and factors which contribute to one being deemed an ineffective use of resources. Amongst factors that Cafcass considered significant to the success of family assistance orders was full agreement by the parties to the order and the purpose of the order. In addition, if the parties agree to an arrangement in principle, but are unable to offer the additional support that the child needs in order to start/ progress that arrangement, a family assistance order may be the answer. On the other hand, Cafcass are clear that in cases involving hostile or entrenched parents, which have not progressed sufficiently well throughout other intervention, such as the involvement of a rule 16.4 guardian (see below) or a section 7 report, and where work could have been completed as part of these measures, a family assistance order may not be appropriate. In particular, it should not be considered when other routes have been tried and failed; a family assistance order is not the last order to try on a menu of options.[193] [194]

---

[189] PD12M, para. 1.2

[190] ibid., para. 1.4

[191] ibid., para. 1.5

[192] Cafcass, *Family Assistance Order Guidance,* (https://www.cafcass.gov.uk/wp-content/uploads/2017/12/Family-Assistance-Orders-guidance-flow-chart.pdf)

[193] ibid., page. 3

[194] For a previous decision in which a family assistance order had not been effective in supporting positive contact arrangements for the children, and the court decided it would not make a further family assistance order, see *B & C (Children: Child Arrangements Order)* [2018] EWFC B100.

Examples

In the matter of *Re L and M (Children: Private Law),*[195] Pauffley J was concerned with a family that lived in Israel during the parents' marriage, but in which the mother had been given permission to relocate to England with the children (aged 13 and 9) with extensive provision of indirect contact as well as direct staying contact three times per year in Israel with the father. There had been no contact with the father for over a year. The court ultimately concluded that the mother had not manipulated the children and alienated them in this case, and was critical of the father's lack of sensitivity and insight to the children's needs, including his tone in correspondence. The guardian recommended no direct contact. She considered that to enforce direct contact would leave the children feeling scared and anxious, and have a detrimental impact upon their well-being. Upon making an order for indirect contact, the court also made a twelve-month family assistance order. The Cafcass officer had agreed to assist the father in the exercise of writing suitable letters to the children.

In *Re Y (A Child) (Private Law),*[196] Pauffley J, having made an interim transfer of residence from the mother to the father following unfounded allegations of abuse, including sexual abuse against the father,[197] considered the mother's contact with the parties' two-year old daughter going forwards. The court determined that contact at its current level of twice per week was unsustainable and was affecting the child's welfare. Contact was therefore to be gradually scaled down to fortnightly intervals. The fortnightly arrangement was to remain until the mother and her relatives made progress in accepting the father as the person responsible for meeting the child's daily needs, and until she had altered her fixed and unshakeable belief system relating to the danger posed by the father. In making a family assistance order, Pauffley J concluded:

> *"27. No one resists the making of a Family Assistance Order pursuant to s. 16 of the Act as amended. Had it been the case that YA could have*

[195] [2014] EWHC 939 (Fam)

[196] [2014] EWHC 2815 (Fam)

[197] The previous decision of *Re Y (A Child) (Private Law: Interim Change of Residence)* [2014] EWHC 1068 (Fam) is considered in **Chapter 7: Transfers of residence**

remained as the allocated worker throughout the next 12 months then I might well have inclined towards leaving the authority to fulfil its obligations to Y on the basis of the Child in Need Plan. Because her considerable talents will be needed in other cases and accordingly at some stage there will a change to the long term team, it seems to me that it would be altogether appropriate to make a Family Assistance Order directing the authority to make available an officer to advise, assist and befriend both parents – each consent to being named – as well as Y herself.

28. The second authority will be in no doubt as to where the focus of attention should be – it is upon the need for advice and assistance in relation to improving and maintaining the mother's contact with Y. Pivotal in that will be the hoped for improvement in how the parents relate to one another as well as attitudinal change amongst maternal family members."

The court directed very brief reports at three, six and twelve month intervals. However these were not for the purpose of monitoring developments, but for the parents to know how the officer considered progress is, or is not, being maintained.

Enforcement of child arrangements orders

It is recognised that it is common in cases in which a child is hostile towards contact for interim child arrangements to lead to all sorts of difficulties. Whether it is the child allegedly voting with their feet and refusing to leave the resident parents' house, or problems manifesting at handovers, problems will invariably arise. The response of the resident parent can be instrumental in helping to manage this, however in cases involving alienation this can often not be relied upon for obvious reasons.

The temptation can be for the court to row back from interim child arrangements orders. As Munby J notes however in *Re D (Intractable Contact Dispute: Publicity),*[198]arguments to this effect, which most

[198] [2007] EWHC 727 (Fam)

frequently will be advanced by the resident parent (although potentially by the children's guardian too), should be treated with caution:

> "[...] *Finally, although this point is in fact absolutely central to the father's complaints, there is the characteristic judicial response when difficulties with contact emerged: reduce the amount of contact and replace unsupervised with supervised contact. The original consent order made on 27 November 1998 provided for the father to have over seven hours unsupervised contact each weekend. Difficulties emerge: in plain language, the mother obstructs contact. On 7 June 1999 the contact is reduced to two hours at a contact centre. On 19 January 2000, and again on 12 April 2000, orders are made providing for unsupervised contact for three hours. Mother obstructs contact. On 26 April 2000 a suspended committal order is made. On 12 May 2000 the contact is again reduced to two hours at a contact centre.*"[199]

In other words, as opposed to taking the more difficult route, and dealing with the resident parents' defiance of its orders, the court retreats and does not enforce its own orders. The approach the court adopts is ultimately a careful balancing exercise, and the factor which nearly always runs counter to the argument to continue with the interim arrangements is the distress such arrangements are causing to the child.

<u>Warning notices</u>

Pursuant to section 11I of the 1989 Act, whenever the court makes or varies a child arrangements order, it is to attach a notice warning of the consequences of failing to comply. These may be an enforcement order for unpaid work (sections 11J – 11N), an order for financial compensation (sections 11O – 11P), or the use of the court's sanctions for contempt.

[199] ibid., para. 21(viii)

Procedure for applying for enforcement

An application for enforcement of a child arrangements order is made by Form C79. The procedure for applying to enforce a child arrangements order is set out in PD12B, paragraph 21.

On application for enforcement of a child arrangements order, the court shall:

i. Consider whether the facts relevant to the alleged non-compliance are agreed, or whether it is necessary to conduct a hearing to establish the facts;

ii. Consider the reasons for any non-compliance;

iii. Consider how the wishes and feelings of the child are to be ascertained;

iv. Consider whether advice is required from Cafcass / Cafcass Cymru on the appropriate way forward;

v. Assess and manage any risks of making further or other child arrangements order;

vi. Consider whether a SPIP or referral for dispute resolution is appropriate;

vii. Consider whether an enforcement order may be appropriate; and

viii. Consider the welfare checklist.[200]

The Gatekeepers shall list any application for enforcement for hearing, before the previously allocated judge if possible, within 20 working days of issue. Enforcement cases should be conducted without delay for reasons which will be self-evident.[201] (Explored more fully in **Chapter 4:**

---

[200] PD12B, para. 21.1

[201] PD12B, para. 21.2

Procedurally managing cases involving allegations of parental alienation).

The Gatekeepers shall also consider and direct if necessary that further safeguarding checks are requested from Cafcass/Cafcass Cymru. In circumstances where an application for enforcement is issued more than three months after the order which is subject to enforcement was made, safeguarding checks shall be ordered by default.[202]

In all enforcement cases, the court will be looking at whether there has been a breach of the child arrangements order *without reasonable excuse*.[203] As well as referral to a SPIP (or in Wales WT4C) or mediation, or variation of the child arrangements order (which could include a more defined order and/ or reconsideration of the contact arrangements or living arrangements), the court has a number of powers available to it.[204] The latter can be sufficient in the event that there is, for example, a dispute about the meaning of the terms of an order.

The Cafcass Guidance notes that the court has a discretion to join the child as a party to enforcement proceedings, and the child is not automatically a party even when a party to the original proceedings. It will rarely be necessary in practice. However, if necessary, the Cafcass officer can be asked to consider this and provide their opinion.[205]

Enforcement orders (sections 11J – 11N of the 1989 Act)

Where the court is satisfied beyond reasonable doubt that a person has failed to comply with a child arrangements order, it may make an enforcement order which imposes on that person an 'unpaid work requirement' (of between 40 and 200 hours, pursuant to Schedule A1 Part 1 of the 1989 Act, para. 3B(1)) pursuant to section 11J(2) of the 1989 Act.

---

[202] PD12B, para. 21.4

[203] PD12B, para. 21.5

[204] PD12B, para. 21.6

[205] Cafcass Guidance on s11A-P, para. 4.1

In the event that an order under this section is pursued, the court must determine the facts in order to establish the cause of the alleged failure to comply, and whether the party allegedly in breach had a 'reasonable excuse' for breaching the order (section 11J(3)).[206] The burden for providing and proving a reasonable excuse is on the person who has allegedly breached the order, and the standard of proof is the balance of probabilities (section 11J(4)).

It should be noted that section 11J(3), concerning 'reasonable excuse', is only relevant once a failure to comply with the terms of the order has been identified, and the question of whether there has been a failure to comply or a breach cannot be determined by reference to 'reasonable excuse.' Munby LJ (as he then was) notes in the Court of Appeal in *Re L-W (Enforcement and Committal: Contact)*[207]:

> "*I should add a few words about what is meant by 'reasonable excuse'. Bearing in mind that a defendant is not in breach of a mandatory order, even if he has not done what the order required, if it was not within his power to do it, issues of force majeure are properly to be considered as going to questions of breach rather than reasonable excuse. So, for example, if a parent taking a child for contact is prevented from going on or is delayed by unforeseen and insuperable transport or weather problems – one thinks of the sudden and unexpected grounding of the nation's airlines by volcanic ash – then there will be no breach. Reasonable excuse, in contrast, arises where, although it was within the power of the defendant to comply, he has some good reason, specifically, a 'reasonable excuse', for not doing so. A typical case might be where a child suddenly falls ill and the defendant, reasonably in the circumstances, takes the child to the doctor rather than going to contact.*"[208]

The court is unable to make an enforcement order unless the person allegedly in breach of the child arrangements order has been given a copy of, or otherwise informed of the terms of (a) in the case of a failure to comply with a provision of a child arrangements order where the order

[206] See PD12B, para. 21.7

[207] [2010] EWCA Civ 1253

[208] ibid., para. 40

was varied before the failure occurred, a notice under section 11I relating to the variation or, where more than one such order has been made, the last order preceding the failure in question, or (b) in any other case, a notice under section 11I relating to the child arrangements order (section 11K)).

In determining whether to make an enforcement order, the court must consider the factors as set out in section 11L of the 1989 Act. This includes the court being satisfied pursuant to section 11L(1) that:

a. Making the enforcement order proposed is necessary to secure the person's compliance with the child arrangements order or any child arrangements order that has effect in its place;

b. The likely effect on the person of the enforcement order proposed to be made is proportionate to the seriousness of the breach.

Further, the court must satisfy itself that provision for the person to work can be made in the local justice area in which the person in breach resides (section 11L(2)), the likely effect of the enforcement order upon them (section 11L(3)), including any conflict with religious beliefs and any interference with times (if any) at which they work or attend an educational establishment (section 11(4)). The court can ask a Cafcass officer to provide information in respect of these matters, for example Cafcass will be able to liaise with the National Probation Service ('NPS') in order to determine the local availability of unpaid work (although leave of the court will be required to disclose as much information as is necessary about the case to the NPS for this to be possible).[209]

Perhaps most crucially, the welfare of the child must be taken into account (section 11(7)). Cafcass will be able to advise on this, however it should be noted that the child's welfare is not the court's paramount consideration.[210]

The court may also ask that a Cafcass officer monitors, or arranges for the monitoring of, a person's compliance with an enforcement order, and

[209] Cafcass Guidance on s11A-P, para. 4.2

[210] See Cafcass Guidance on s11A-P, para. 4.2

to report to the court on their failure (if any) to comply (without reasonable excuse) and on any unsuitability to undertake the unpaid work (section 11M). This monitoring of compliance with unpaid work requirements is generally undertaken by the NPS, on a similar basis to that followed with those referred to it by the criminal courts. The Cafcass officer will therefore need to notify the NPS, which in turn will report to Cafcass on compliance.[211]

The court should also attach a warning notice to any enforcement order that is made, and this should set out the consequences of breaching the enforcement order (section 11N). Not only will this include a warning that proceedings can be brought for contempt of court (see below), but the court can also amend the original order in order to extend it to make it more onerous, or impose another enforcement order (Schedule A1, Part 2).

Financial compensation orders (section 11O – 11P of the 1989 Act)

The court also has the power to make a financial compensation order. It can do so if satisfied that an individual has failed to comply with a provision of a child arrangements order, and that a person whose contact with the child concerned is provided for within the order (or who otherwise falls within section 11O(6)) has suffered financial loss by reason of the breach (section 11O(2)).

In the event that an order under this section is pursued, the court must determine the facts in order to establish the cause of the alleged failure to comply, and whether the party allegedly in breach had a 'reasonable excuse' for breaching the order (section 11O(3)).[212]

The child concerned is able to make such an application for compensation for financial loss (section 11O(6)(d)) with leave of the court (section 11O(7)). That permission will only be granted if the child has sufficient understanding (section 11O(8)).

211 Cafcass Guidance on s11A-P, para. 4.3

212 See PD12B, para. 21.7

While the amount of compensation payable by the individual in breach may not exceed the amount of the applicant's financial loss (section 11O(9)), such an order can be extremely useful in circumstances where, for example, contact centre costs have been incurred, or, in more extreme circumstances, travel/holiday costs.

The court is under a statutory duty to take into account the financial circumstances of the individual in breach (section 11O(10)). As with enforcement orders, while the court must take into account the welfare of the child concerned (section 11(14), the welfare of the child is not the court's paramount consideration. Cafcass is unlikely to be aware of applications for financial compensation orders. However, it is possible that the court will seek information from Cafcass about the welfare of the child for this purpose.[213]

It is notable that the court may not however make an order for financial compensation where the person in breach did not receive a warning notice under section 11I, and was not otherwise informed of its terms (section 11P).

Contempt of court

The court's sanctions for contempt of court include, for example, fining an individual who is in breach of a child arrangements order, sequestration of their assets, or committing them to prison. It is perhaps the most extreme and severe form of enforcement. There is a dual purpose to any committal application: to punish for breach, and to ensure future compliance with the terms of the order.

In committal proceedings, the standard of proof is the criminal standard: the court must be satisfied beyond reasonable doubt that the defendant breached the terms of the order. The burden of proof is on the applicant.

The procedure in relation to applications and proceedings for committal for contempt of court is outside the scope of this Chapter, however, is governed by the FPR 2010 Part 37, and PD37A. It is merely noted that

[213] Cafcass Guidance on s11A-P, para. 5.1

there have been a number of cases[214] where the importance of avoiding serious procedural irregularities in committal proceedings has been emphasised. These parts of the FPR 2010 are important therefore, and should be adhered to thoroughly.

It is also important to note that a penal notice, which warns the person against whom the order was made that failure to obey the contents of the child arrangements order constitutes a contempt of court, and may have the consequences as outlined above, must be attached to order that is alleged to have been breached in order for proceedings to be brought (see FPR 2010, r.37.4(e)). The order must be clear and unambiguous in specifying what must be done or must not be done. The order with the penal notice must have also been personally served upon the defendant, unless the court is otherwise satisfied that they had notice of the terms of the order or service is dispensed with.

The following important principles should also be kept in mind when seeking enforcement, in particular by way of committal.

The first is in respect of the impact of the consequences of committal upon the child, and the potential to do further damage to the relationship between the non-resident parent and the child.

The case of *Re L-W (Enforcement and Committal: Contact)*[215] is an important reminder of this. It concerned protracted proceedings in relation to a boy, aged 10. An order was in place requiring the father to allow the mother to have contact with him one Saturday afternoon every four weeks. After two failed attempts, the mother brought proceedings for an enforcement order, and an order for compensation for financial loss for her petrol costs. A further hearing saw an increase in contact ordered, however these subsequent attempts failed too, and the trial judge made two enforcement orders imposing a total of 200 hours of unpaid work on the father, three compensation orders intending to remunerate the mother for her financial losses, and a committal order. The trial judge

---

[214] See, for example, *CH v CT (Committal: Appeal)* [2018] EWHC 1310 (Fam).

[215] [2010] EWCA Civ 1253

held the father was obliged to exercise effective parental control over his son, and it was not enough for him to say that he did not want to go.

On appeal, the Court of Appeal considered that the welfare of the child was a material consideration, but not paramount. Although it regarded committal as an essential weapon in the court's armoury in intractable contact disputes, and that it could be an appropriate way of enforcing an order, it should not be used unless it is a "*proportionate response to problem nor if some less drastic remedy will provide an adequate solution.*"[216] The court considered the benefits of bringing committal proceedings early, suggesting:

> "[...] *this does not mean that one has to wait unduly before having resort to committal, let alone waiting so long that the moment has passed and the situation has become irretrievable. That point, in the nature of things, is often easier to identify with the priceless benefit of hindsight – I do not underestimate the difficulties of deciding the right strategy in this kind of case. But I cannot help feeling that, on occasions, the understandable reluctance to resort to such a drastic remedy as committal means that when recourse to it is first proposed it is too late for committal, whereas a willingness to grasp the nettle by making a committal order at an earlier stage might have ended up making all the difference. I repeat a point I have already made. The threat, or if need be the actual implementation, of a very short period of imprisonment – just a day or two – may at an earlier stage of the proceedings achieve more than the threat of a longer sentence at a much later stage in the process. I do not suggest this as a panacea – this is an area in which there is no panacea – but it is something which, I suggest, is worth keeping in mind.*"[217]

However, in the instant case, the Court of Appeal concluded that committal of the father to prison would simply be "*counterproductive*" and the committal order could not stand for this reason.[218] It was clear that the court needed to consider, if the child had internalised the resident parent's hostility, that punishing that parent may not produce

[216] ibid., para. 108

[217] ibid.

[218] ibid., para. 107

the intended outcome and may in fact produce the opposite effect.[219] As Sedley LJ observed: "*The premise on which the judge made his initial order has become absorbed into a much more complex and intractable situation which punishing the father not only cannot solve but will exacerbate.*"[220]

This has been similarly noted in by Bracewell J in *V v V (Contact: Implacable Hostility)*[221] (considered further in **Chapter 7: Transfers of residence**). In respect of orders to send a parent to prison, or to make a suspended order of imprisonment, Bracewell J notes: "*This option may well not achieve the object of reinstating contact; the child may blame the parent who applied to commit the carer to prison; the child's life may be disrupted if there is no one capable of or willing to care for the child when the parent is in prison; it cannot be anything other than emotionally damaging for a child to be suddenly removed into foster care by social services from a parent, usually a mother, who in all respects except contact is a good parent.*"[222]

The second principle is the difficulty in establishing breach of the child arrangements order. It was made clear in *Re L-W (Enforcement and Committal: Contact)* that a parent's obligation to 'allow' contact or 'make the child available' for contact, does not place them in breach of the order in the event of a child's refusal to co-operate. The father in this case was not under a legally enforceable duty to take such steps in the exercise of parental discipline, and, in fact, guidance and encouragement were considered reasonable in the circumstances to ensure contact took place. Munby LJ (as he then was) noted:

> *"The father's obligations under each successive order were to 'allow' contact and 'make M available' for contact. To 'allow' is to concede or to permit; to 'make available' is to put at one's disposal or within one's reach. That was the father's obligation; no more and no less. But that is not how Judge Caddick treated the orders. Running through all his judgments is the assumption, indeed the repeated assertion (see the passages I have set out in paras [26], [51], [61], [67] and [68] above),*

[219] ibid., para. 123

[220] ibid., para. 122

[221] [2004] EWHC 1215 (Fam)

[222] ibid., para. 10

that the father's obligation was to 'make sure' or 'ensure' that M went and that contact took place. The father's obligation, according to Judge Caddick (see the passage set out in para [61] above), was to 'make sure that he did all that was necessary so that that child would go' and to take 'whatever other steps within the exercise of his parental responsibility were necessary to make sure that he went'. The father may have been under a parental or moral obligation to do these things, but on the wording of these orders he was not, in my judgment, under any legal obligation such as to render him in breach of the orders for failing to do them, let alone for failing to achieve – to 'ensure' – that contact actually took place. Nor, with all respect to Mr Walden-Smith, was the father under a legally enforceable obligation to take such steps in the exercise of his parental discipline, guidance and encouragement as were reasonable in all the circumstances to ensure that contact took place."[223]

The implications are clear, in particular in circumstances of alienation where the child's objection *is* often the reason contact does not take place, albeit as a result of parental influence. In such circumstances, it appears in many cases the alienating parent has a clear defence to use as a shield that can make it challenging to get enforcement proceedings off the ground.

Therapeutic intervention

A starting point in many cases is to adopt a therapeutic approach to re-establishing a relationship between the child and the non-resident parent. Indeed, judges such as HHJ Wildblood QC in *Re A (Children) (Parental alienation)*[224] (considered in **Chapter 4: Procedurally managing cases involving allegations of parental alienation**) have noted the challenges that can present if the extent of both the child's emotional and psychological issues are not identified early, and therapeutic intervention does not follow quickly thereafter.[225]

---

[223] *Re L-W (Enforcement and Committal: Contact)* [2010] EWCA Civ 1253, para. 76

[224] [2019] 9 WLUK 445

[225] ibid., para. 13(viii)

The benefits of the therapy, as with nearly all approaches available to the court, are nonetheless not universally endorsed by all experts. Once more there is no 'one-size-fits-all' approach, and the merits of a therapeutic approach will need to be assessed in the context of the child's resistance, the stage proceedings have reached, how capable the alienating parent is of changing, and whether it has been tried and failed previously (amongst other factors).

Further, while approaches may differ, it is unlikely that a course of therapy will be recommended in cases where a child is not agreeable to it. In *F v M & Ors*[226], the expert in the case Dr Mark Berelowitz (child and adolescent psychiatrist) said that while it may be reasonable for the child to attend joint sessions with a parent to work on the issues relating to that parent, it would be unreasonable to force a child to go to therapy alone to which she did not agree to. Nonetheless, in evaluating whether such work was to take place with the child and the alienating parent, it was recommended that it should not be endorsed unless the court was confident to a "*high degree*" that the alienating parent can "*be relied upon unequivocally and wholeheartedly to support the work and that furthermore his other actions do not pull X [the child] in the opposite direction.*"[227]. In this case, the court did not have the requisite confidence in the father.

The way that therapy can be approached will differ from case-to-case. In some cases, it is beneficial for the child alone to engage with therapy. Other models will adopt a family therapy model which can involve work both in an individual capacity and as a family-unit. A review of the techniques and methods that can be employed in such cases is beyond the scope of this book, however different experts will employ different methods of practice.

Examples

In the decision of *Re S (Transfer of Residence)*[228] (also considered in **Chapter 7: Transfers of residence**) HHJ Bellamy reflected upon some of the diverse approaches to therapy as a means of resolving a case involving

---

[226] [2021] EWFC 18

[227] ibid., para. 202-203

[228] [2010] EWHC B19 (Fam)

a child (S) who has been alienated. There was divergent opinion between Karen Woodall (psychotherapist) and Dr Weir (child and adult psychiatrist) as to the benefits of a continuing therapeutic approach in unlocking the situation that had prevailed in which an order for a transfer of residence had been made in respect of a child who was refusing to have any sort of relationship with his father as a result of alienation. The transfer of residence failed, and the child ended up returning to live with the mother from the foster care placement he had been residing in as an interim holding position with the father's consent.

After the child returned to live with the mother, therapeutic work was set up between the parents and the child. Ms Woodall led the work:

> *"29. Mrs Woodall explained the approach she proposed to take:*
>
> > *'9.1 My proposal for continued work with this case is influenced by the multi model approach developed by Johnston, Walters and Friedlander in 2001. This is a multi faceted intervention that is inclusive of all the family members and matches the intervention to the nature of the problem.'*
>
> *30. The initial stage of this approach involved intensive therapeutic work with the parents and S, to include weekly therapeutic contact sessions. Between 8 June and 1 July Mrs Woodall undertook a total of thirteen therapeutic sessions lasting almost 24 hours in total. S was involved in five of these sessions. In addition, Mrs Woodall facilitated three direct contact sessions between S and his father.*
>
> *31. In her second report Mrs Woodall says that she detected small but, in her opinion, significant signs of progress. She reports that she had 'observed and facilitated contact between [the father] and S' and had 'observed that S does listen, does respond in body language and, during the last session was extremely tentatively, able to begin to discuss issues with his father using me as a bridge'. She noted that S 'is able to talk about when not if he reunites with his father'.*
>
> *32. Mrs Woodall made the point that this approach to working with the family is 'an alternative treatment to that of a change of residence' and not one which can run alongside change of residence. She states*

that this approach requires a minimum of six to twelve months for successful implementation 'and should be reviewed by the judge who is case managing at agreed intervals'. She was very clear that the father's wish to implement the order that S should move to live with him must be abandoned. Her proposed programme for the next three months involved further intensive work with the parents and S."

Karen Woodall's approach was however not supported by the other expert in the case. Dr Weir, who had recommended the transfer of residence and advised the court on how it might be implemented, did not agree that a therapeutic approach would succeed in these sorts of cases. HHJ Bellamy noted:

> "[…] *Throughout the course of his evidence Dr Weir has held strongly to the view that serious cases of alienation are unlikely to be resolved by means of therapy. In his final report he says:*
>
> > *'I do not share Ms Woodall's optimism that further therapeutic intervention will succeed... This is a serious and entrenched case of alienation...and it has been and remains my opinion that therapy is unlikely to succeed in overcoming S's resistance to any form of relationship with his father's family.'"*[229]

Ultimately, the father agreed not only to withdraw his application to implement the transfer of residence, but that further intensive therapeutic work was not in the child's welfare interests given the difficulties over the past months and the deterioration in the child's mental health. HHJ Bellamy agreed:

> *"53. Therapy had already been tried in this case. It began in August 2006 and was ongoing at the time of the first contested hearing before me in November 2007. The two therapists had been instructed in the hope that therapy would, in due course, lead to the restoration of direct contact between father and son. The therapists had no experience of working with families in high conflict cases or, more importantly, of*

[229] ibid., para. 33

working with alienated children. That therapy failed to achieve its objective.

54. There is no doubt that Mrs Woodall has the experience which the earlier therapists lacked. However, despite the intensive work she undertook in June the progress made was extremely modest. Mrs Woodall herself described the progress as 'tiny'. In the light of the report from CAHMS it is difficult to see how the court could have come to the conclusion that the intensive regime of further therapy proposed by Mrs Woodall would have been in the best interests of S's welfare."

In this case, a decisive factor was that therapy had been tried and failed. Ultimately, therapy will never be a 'one-size-fits-all' solution to dealing with an alienated child in a high conflict case. Professional opinion may differ in respect of its merits, and case specific factors may make it the right or wrong approach. It is however a tool that is available in the right sort of case.

Whilst therapeutic intervention can be a positive means of trying to make progress before more drastic alternatives are considered, consideration can also be given as to how therapy may work *alongside* other measures. Again, professional opinion on the benefits of this will differ, and each case should be considered on its own facts.

In the decision of *Re A and B (Parental Alienation: No. 1)*[230] (considered further in **Chapter 7: Transfers of residence**), the court noted that prior to ordering a transfer of residence, there had already been a programme of work designed to rectify the parental alienation and seek to ensure the children had a relationship with their father. The programme lasted for some 15-months. This work was carried out by Karen Woodall (psychotherapist), working collaboratively with Dr Janine Braier (psychologist). It was this programme of work which proved crucial in underpinning the expert reports and recommendations on how to progress the case when the matter came before Keehan J in November 2020. Ms Woodall described how she and Dr Braier had been "*constantly engaged in crisis management and firefighting*"[231], and doubted that after

[230] [2020] EWHC 3366 (Fam)

[231] ibid., para. 28

this 15-month programme of work the mother could make any more progress. It was on this basis that it was concluded by both Dr Braier and Karen Woodall that further work to support a 50/50 shared care arrangement was simply not warranted.[232] Keehan J ultimately concluded a transfer of residence was in these children's welfare interests, albeit with further therapeutic work to be undertaken *alongside* the transfer.

In *Re A and B (Parental Alienation: No. 2)*[233] Keehan J noted how upon transferring the children's residence in this case he had also made an order for further therapeutic intervention by Karen Woodall. The aim of such therapy was to improve the prospects of the transfer succeeding by attempting to repair the emotional damage the children had suffered, assisting the children in settling in with their father, and helping the mother in understanding the role she had played and the harm she had caused to the children. Ultimately, the transfer was unsuccessful. However Karen Woodall's work during and after the failed transfer provided an insight to for the court in respect of why this had been the case:

> *"12. By her acts to date and by her conduct of this litigation since my judgment in November, I am in no doubt and find that the mother has done everything that she can to frustrate my judgment, to frustrate the placement of the children with the father, and to frustrate the reparative therapeutic work that Ms Woodall has been doing. She has constantly gone to her solicitors who have raised questions about the approach of Ms Woodall. Ms Woodall has noted that the mother either does not understand what Ms Woodall is saying to her or she does not accept what Ms Woodall is advising her to do in the therapeutic process. In those circumstances, as was raised in the previous hearing by both Dr Braier and Ms Woodall, Ms Woodall questioned whether the mother had reached the ceiling of the change and insight that she is able to effect.*

[232] ibid., para. 28-35

[233] [2021] EWHC 2601 (Fam)

13. I have no confidence, on the totality of the evidence before me, that this mother has engaged with the therapeutic process so as to reflect on her past behaviour and to consider how she can change. It is plain beyond peradventure, as set out in my earlier judgment, that this mother caused serious and deep emotional harm to the children. However, both at the substantive final hearing and now, I can evince no evidence that she acknowledges or accepts the harm she caused the children and I can evince no evidence that she is making any real progress to change. Absent that recognition and absent that change, it is very difficult to see how, safely and in the welfare best interests of the children, contact in any form can be resumed."

In the end, as noted in the fourth judgment, *Re A and B (Parental Alienation: No. 4)*[234], the transfer of residence was successful. The court praised the father and his wife, but also Karen Woodall for the guidance she had given over a number of months and for being key to ensuring the children were able to have a relationship with their father. Her continuing involvement and therapeutic support was not simply a way for the court to see what was happening 'on-the-ground', but also essential in the long-term success of the transfer.

Wardship

While comparatively rare, another possibility in intractable child arrangement disputes is for the court to make the child a ward of court. In essence, the court becomes the child's 'official parents' and assume power over major decisions concerning the child's life. In practical terms, this means that no important step can be taken in the child's life without leave of the court. This can have immense benefits in intractable cases where the court's intervention is required in day-to-day decision making.

In a recent case before the High Court, *Re T (Parental Alienation)*[235], the father applied for the transfer of residence for his five-year-old daughter. The court had made findings of parental alienation. In that case an application had been made at a previous hearing before Moor J for the child to be made a ward on the basis that the local authority was taking

---

[234] [2021] EWHC 2603 (Fam)

[235] [2019] EWHC 3854 (Fam)

no further action in respect of the family, and proceedings had been ongoing for some years, with little progress. At the end of the proceedings before Judge Raeside QC, the wardship was discharged, and a child arrangements order was made that the child should live with the father with such contact with the mother as may be agreed in consultation, in the first instance, with children's services.

It is clear from this case that, whilst wardship applications are rare, they still serve an important purpose in private children cases where there have been findings of parental alienation.[236]

[236] With thanks to Moore Barlow Lawyers, 'Using wardship for intractable child arrangements disputes', 18 May 2020 (https://www.moorebarlow.com/using-wardship-for-intractable-child-arrangement-disputes/)

CHAPTER SIX

THE VOICE OF THE CHILD

Basic Principles

The importance of hearing children

It is a fundamental principle of our domestic and international procedure that in proceedings relating to children, the court should consider whether and how to hear the voice of the child.[237] In particular, since the decision of the House of Lords in *Re D (A Child) (Abduction: Rights of Custody)*[238], there has been a growing understanding of the need to 'hear' children in proceedings concerning them:

> *"As any parent who has ever asked a child what he wants for tea knows, there is a large difference between taking account of a child's views and doing what he wants. But there is now a growing understanding of the importance of listening to the children involved in children's cases. It is the child, more than anyone else, who will have to live with what the court decides. Those who do listen to children understand that they often have a point of view which is quite distinct from that of the person looking after them. They are quite capable of being moral actors in their own right. Just as the adults may have to do what the court decides whether they like it or not, so may the child. But that is no more a reason for failing to hear what the child has to say than it is for refusing to hear the parent's views."*[239]

---

[237] See *Re D (A Child) (Abduction: Rights of Custody)* [2006] UKHL 51; *Re D (A Child) (Recognition of Foreign Order) (Reunite Child Abduction Centre Intervening)* [2016] EWCA Civ 12; Article 12 of the UNCRC

[238] [2006] UKHL 51

[239] ibid. para. 57

The importance of hearing the voice of the child is reflected in the wording of The United Nations Convention on the Rights of the Child 1989 ('UNCRC'). Article 12 requires that *"the child who is capable of forming his or her own views be assured the right to express these views freely in all matters effecting the child, the views of the child being given due weight in accordance with the age and maturity of the child."* In particular this must include the opportunity to be heard in any judicial and administrative proceedings affecting the child.

In *Mabon v Mabon*[240] the Court of Appeal held that the time had come to recognise the growing importance of the acknowledgement of autonomy and consequential rights of children both nationally and internationally, and particularly under the UNCRC and ECHR. In reaching his judgment Thorpe LJ concluded as follows:

> *"Unless we in this jurisdiction are to fall out of step with similar societies as they safeguard Art 12 rights, we must, in the case of articulate teenagers, accept that the right to freedom of expression and participation outweighs the paternalistic judgment of welfare."*[241]

<u>The weight given to the child's voice</u>

In circumstances where the court is considering whether to make, vary or discharge a section 8 order under the 1989 Act, section 1(3)(a) of the 1989 Act requires the court to have regard to *"the ascertainable wishes and feelings of the child concerned (considered in light of his age and understanding)."*

The importance of age and understanding must be emphasised. In *Re R (Residence Order)*[242], the Court of Appeal noted in particular that courts must be careful not to discount the wishes and feelings (and the reasons behind them) of mature children as against other welfare factors. As far as age was concerned, Rix LJ reiterated the views of Dame Elizabeth Butler-Sloss P in *Re L, Re V, Re M and Re H (Contact: Domestic*

240 [2005] EWCA Civ 634

241 ibid. para. 28

242 [2009] EWCA Civ 445

Violence)[243], where she quoted approvingly the following words from Drs Sturges and Glaser's report:[244]

> *"... the older the child the more seriously they should be viewed and the more insulting and discrediting to the child to have them ignored. As a rough rule we would see these as needing to be taken account of at any age; above 10 we see these as carrying considerable weight with 6–10 as an intermediate stage and at under 6 as often indistinguishable in many ways from the wishes of the main carer (assuming normal development). In domestic violence, where the child has memories of that violence we would see their wishes as warranting much more weight than in situations where no real reason for the child's resistance appears to exist."*

Whilst of course it is a fundamental principle that the child who is subject to the proceedings shall be heard, the manner and the degree to which the child is heard varies on a case by case basis. The 'welfare checklist' at section 1(3) of the 1989 Act is subject to the overarching requirement at section 1(1) that the welfare of the child must be the paramount consideration of the court.

Judges will be informed of a child's wishes and feelings through a number of methods, most commonly within a report under the section 7 of the 1989 Act, prepared by a social worker or Cafcass FCA and, in the context of children who have been joined to proceedings, through their guardian. Expert assessments by psychiatrists and psychologists can add further understanding to what the child is feeling towards the non-resident parent, including non-verbal cues and behaviours. The child's wishes and feelings are frequently provided to the court through a third party professional therefore, shaped in part by the questions that that professional has posed to the child and the assessment that they have made about what the child is telling them. The judge must in turn determine the extent to which the professionals' assessment of the child's expressed wishes and feelings should be accepted – in other words use all the information before them to reach their own assessment as to the

243 [2000] EWCA Civ 194; [2002] 2 FLR 334

244 Drs Glaser and Sturges, 'Contact and domestic violence: the experts court report', [2000] Fam Law 615

weight to accord to the child's wishes and feelings. Thereafter, a conclusion will be reached as to the impact such an assessment has upon any welfare decision the judge has to make.

This exercise is of course complicated in cases involving allegations of parental alienation. The assessments which both the third-party professional is making and, in turn, the judge is undertaking are about the degree to which the child's *expressed* wishes and feelings represent the child's *true* wishes and feelings.

As put by HHJ Wildblood QC in *Re A (Children) (Parental alienation)*[245] (considered in **Chapter 4: Procedurally managing cases involving allegations of parental alienation**):

> *"There is an obvious difficulty about how to approach the expressed wishes and feelings of children who are living in an alienating environment such as this. If children who have been alienated are asked whether they wish to have a relationship with the non-resident parent there is a likelihood that the alienation they have experienced will lead them to say 'no.' Therefore, in this type of case, the approach to the wishes and feelings of children has had to be approached with considerable care and professionalism. To respond simply on the basis of what children say in this type of situation is manifestly superficial and naive. The children in this case have been expressing wishes that they should not see their father for many years now. The lack of an effective and early enquiry into what was happening within this family meant that there was no effective intervention. That, in turn, has led to the children's expressed wishes being reinforced in their minds. It has also resulted in the mother being able to say 'we should listen to the children', rather than addressing the underlying difficulties."*[246]

If an alienated child's views are treated as determinative of the outcome, the court would simply be giving effect to the alienating parent's desired outcome. Alienated children will frequently have become skilled in re-iterating the views of the alienating parent, having learned to say what they think is expected of them. In a recent article entitled 'The Voice of

---

[245] [2019] 9 WLUK 445

[246] ibid., para. 13(ix)

the Child? Listening to Alienated Children'[247], Karen Woodall suggested the following in such situations:

> *"When the child is using the defence of splitting (and all cases of a child's rejection are differentiated for splitting behaviours), the essential task is to compare the child's narrative to that of each parent. A child who is being influenced into an alignment with a parent's beliefs and views of the other parent, will echo the words and phrases and mirror that parent's beliefs. Sometimes this is a subtle mirroring but often it is starkly apparent that the child is not speaking about their own feelings but those which are understood by the child to be the right thing to say and feel."*

The following paragraphs from His Honour Judge Bellamy sitting as a High Court Judge in *Re S (Transfer of Residence)*[248] were endorsed by Thorpe LJ in the Court of Appeal as "*impeccable directions as to how a judge should evaluate the wishes and feelings of a child who has been caught up in terrible conflict…"*[249]*:*

> *"69. A's wishes and feelings must be assessed in accordance with his age and understanding. It is here that the assessment becomes more difficult. I have found that A has become alienated from his father. A has said that his father is a 'monster' and that he 'hates' him. It is clear from Dr Weir's evidence that such behaviour fits within the pattern of behaviour of children who have become alienated from their non-resident parent. In his report of 18th July 2008 Dr Weir was very clear. He said that:*
>
>> *'It is also important for both parents and for all professionals working with the child to recognise that the child's expressed wishes and feelings are irrational and should form no part in the Court's decision making.'*

[247] Karen Woodall, 'The Voice of the Child? Listening to Alienated Children,' 10 July 2020 (https://karenwoodall.blog/2020/07/10/the-voice-of-the-child-listening-to-alienated-children.)

[248] [2010] EWHC 192 (Fam)

[249] *Re S (A Child)* [2010] EWCA Civ 219, para. 28

70. The law requires that the court should take account of A's wishes and feelings. It would be wrong, therefore, for me to pay no regard at all to the views which A has so clearly and consistently expressed. The [Children] Act, the UNCRC and case law all emphasise the importance of listening to and respecting the wishes of the child. As a general proposition I accept that the older the child the greater the respect that should be accorded to his or her wishes and feelings. As Butler Sloss LJ said in re S (Minors) (Access: Religious upbringing) *[1992] 313 at page 321, a case involving two children aged 13 and 11,*

> *'Nobody should dictate to children of this age, because one is dealing with their emotions, their lives and they are not packages to be moved around. They are people entitled to be treated with respect.'*

I cannot and do not ignore A's expressed wishes and feelings. However, in the light of Dr Weir's evidence, it would be equally inappropriate for me to proceed on the basis that those expressed wishes and feelings should necessarily be taken at face value. They need to be assessed in the light of A's age and understanding. The impact of alienation upon the reliability of those wishes and feelings and the signs (albeit modest) that they may not in fact reflect his true feelings, are matters to be taken into account when assessing the weight to be attached to them."

The importance of determining the factual matrix

It is in the context of the above quote that it becomes important (as made clear in **Chapter 4: Procedurally managing cases involving allegations of parental alienation**) to determine the factual matrix underpinning the parties' allegations as soon as possible. As discussed in more detail in **Chapter 3: Parental alienation and domestic abuse**, it is impossible in the context of, for example, competing allegations of domestic abuse and parental alienation to identify if the child's rejection of the non-resident parent is justified or not, and what weight should therefore be given to the child's wishes and feelings as a result.

This point is made by Elizabeth Issacs QC sitting as a Deputy High Court Judge in *F v M & Ors*[250] when assessing the views of Dr Mark Berelowitz (child and adolescent psychiatrist) and the children's guardian, in respect of the children's wishes and feelings in this case. Importantly, this decision post-dated a finding had been made that there had been clear signs of alienation by the father. It is this finding which provided the prism through which the experts could consider the children's wishes and feelings in this case:

> *"144. Dr Berelowitz describes each of the children as expressing different wishes and feelings. It is his expert opinion that the extent to which they have been alienated greatly affects their ascertainable wishes and feelings. Thus, the more the child is alienated, the less their ascertainable wishes and feelings should be taken at face value, and the more need there is for a comprehensive and holistic approach to helping them with their alienation. Put simply, in this case, that would mean that I should pay less regard to X's wishes and feelings about contact with M than I should to those of the other children. Dr Berelowitz also observes that when a child is alienated from one parent, they often become much more dependent on the parent with whom they reside.*
>
> *145. The guardian has extensively consulted the children and sought their views about their living and contact arrangements. He has also had extensive contact with the parents during the period of his involvement. He observes that although at times F asserts that he is just passing on what the children are telling him, in his experience of working with the family in the past two years, it is very difficult to separate F's views from those of the children and at times it seems that F's narrative is so often the same as that of the children. The guardian considers that given the findings of alienation, it is therefore likely that the children's view of M is still being heavily influenced by F. The guardian says that the children's wishes and feelings are not formed in a vacuum, and a question therefore arises as to how much weight should be given to their views. He says –*

[250] [2021] EWFC 18

> *I respect and acknowledge the views expressed by the children, but these views must be seen in the context of their previous experiences and the fact that they have been significantly alienated against their mother.*
>
> *146. The guardian is concerned that if decision-making is led by the children's wishes alone, which is largely what F said he was doing and following between August 2018 and September 2020, they will continue to suffer psychological harm due to alienation from M, which consequently risks further mental health problems as they grow older.*
>
> *147. That analysis is endorsed by Dr Berelowitz, and I accept their combined evidence on this point about how much weight should be attached to the wishes and feelings of alienated children in general, and to these children in particular. Thus the approach I have taken in this case is that the more the child is alienated, the less I should take their ascertainable wishes and feelings at face value, and the more I need to apply a comprehensive and holistic approach to helping them with their alienation."*

It is important to note that, despite an overall finding having been made in respect of alienation, this did not prevent the court from attributing different weight to the children's wishes and feelings in accordance with the extent of their alienation. This ultimately had significant bearing on the welfare analysis. This decision is covered in detail in **Chapter 7: Transfers of residence**, however the options that were before the court included a transfer of *all* the children, or just the two younger children who were less alienated. The strength of the older child's (X) wishes and feelings was part of the reason why, until the father changed his position, the experts concluded it was simply too risky to move the children as a sibling group due to the risk of X undermining the placement for her siblings.

Harm caused by ascertaining wishes and feelings

Whilst the importance of hearing children is clear, in cases involving found or alleged parental alienation, the court must be mindful of the potential for causing further harm to the child, and reinforcing their negative views in respect of the non-resident parent.

The decision of Sir Andrew McFarlane PFD in *Re L (A Child)*[251] highlighted the myriad of complexities that can arise in the wishes and feeling gathering stage. The matter involved an appeal by a mother against an order transferring the residence of the parties' eight-year-old child from his mother's home to his father's home. HHJ Tolson QC had not made findings of intractable hostility or parental alienation, however had found that the father's relationship with the child was being undermined by the mother and maternal grandmother. The child was made subject to proceedings with a children's guardian appointed by Cafcass acting for him, who ultimately recommended a transfer of residence. HHJ Tolson QC held that maintaining the placement with his mother and grandmother would not meet the child's emotional needs and would "*cause him emotional harm in the future.*" The question which arose on appeal of the welfare judgment was whether the guardian and the court had fallen into error in their approach to the child's wishes and feelings. In the context of the fact-finding judgment and the work of her predecessors, the guardian had determined it was not in this child's interests to directly explore with the child his wishes and feelings in respect of a proposed transfer of residence.

Sir Andrew McFarlane PFD in assessing this approach concluded whilst there is:

> *"[...] an express duty placed upon a guardian in a case such as this to report on the child's wishes [...] that duty must be tempered by the overarching requirement to afford paramount consideration to the child's welfare. In the present case, the Guardian began direct work with L which would normally lead to explicit discussion of the central issue before the court. However, during the course of that work she saw first-hand that which her predecessors had also apprehended, namely that this young boy was exquisitely torn between a wholly negative presentation of his father in the maternal home which was in total contradiction to the reality of his relationship with his father when they were seen together. The Guardian considered that any expression of wishes in the current circumstances would be bound to favour the mother. More importantly, she considered that to ask the question and*

[251] [2019] EWHC 867 (Fam)

to put this eight year old boy on the spot of expressing a choice would itself be emotionally harmful. She therefore made the positive decision not to ask him the question. Her decision was, certainly by implication, supported by the solicitors and counsel instructed on L's behalf, who now defend that decision before this court, and her decision was accepted by the very experienced family judge. In those circumstances, it is difficult, indeed it is not possible, for the mother to argue on appeal that the exercise conducted by the Guardian was fatally flawed and that, as a result, the process before the judge should be set aside and a fresh exercise undertaken to canvass L's wishes and feelings."[252]

Sir Andrew McFarlane PFD goes on to consider section 1(3)(a) of the 1989 Act, in particular the meaning of "*ascertainable wishes and feelings*":

"[...] *In the professional opinion of the Guardian, it was not possible to ascertain L's wishes and feelings on the central issue without causing him emotional harm. It was also the view of the Guardian that L's position was such that any expression of wishes would be unlikely to represent his true wishes and feelings, and, to that extent it would not be possible to ascertain the child's genuine view."*[253]

In other words, whilst as a result of the child's negative perception of his father, it would be impossible for the guardian to have ascertained anything other than his expressed wishes and feelings, which would simply have had the effect of amplifying the child's voice as influenced by the maternal family. This would be further to elide either the child's true and unspoken wishes and feelings, or the wishes and feelings he would have expressed in the event he was unencumbered by the maternal family's influence: either way his wishes and feelings were not "*ascertainable*" in any meaningful sense.

A further decision in which the potential for harm was considered is *Re A and B (Parental Alienation: No 2)*[254] (explored further in **Chapter 7: Transfers of residence**). In considering the recommendations of the psychotherapist, Keehan J concluded he would not countenance the

---

[252] ibid., para. 65

[253] ibid., para. 66

[254] [2020] EHWC 3366

children being asked again about what their wishes and feelings were at the point that residence was being transferred. This was in circumstances in which they were "*in the midst of [...] delicate therapeutic work*" and where it "*would be harmful and detrimental to their welfare best interests.*"[255]

Once more, the need for a determination of the factual matrix underpinning the family dynamic is clear. It informs not simply the weight to be attributed to the child's views, but the extent to which the court determines it is even necessary to further ascertain them and the potential harms in doing so.

Joinder and separate representation of children

Joinder of children to proceedings

Whilst the most common method of ascertaining a child's wishes and feelings will be through a section 7 report, in appropriate cases where it is deemed in the best interests of the child to do so, the court is able to join a child to the proceedings and grant them party status.[256]

In *Re LC (Children) (Reunite International Child Abduction Centre Intervening)*[257], which considered the power to order joinder under rule 16.2 (in the context of 1980 Hague Convention proceedings) Lord Wilson described the child's best interests as the 'threshold' condition which opens up the gateway to judicial discretion. But as he also pointed out, this discretion is more theoretical than real, because if a court finds that it is in a child's best interests to be joined, then that will 'almost always' be the result.[258]

In the case of *Ciccone v Ritchie*[259], the judge confirmed that the test for granting party status to a child was whether it was in the child's best interests. Applying that test, a fifteen-year-old boy who strongly opposed

---

[255] ibid., para. 17

[256] FPR 2010, r. 16.2(1)

[257] [2014] UKSC 1

[258] ibid. para. 45

[259] [2016] EWHC 608 (Fam)

having to return to his mother in the US would be joined as a party to the proceedings which his mother had brought under the Hague Convention on the Civil Aspects of International Child Abduction 1980 ('1980 Hague Convention'). To confine him to a passive role would not be in his best interests.

It is important to note that all the judicial guidance states that the decision as to whether or not the child ought to be joined as a party to proceedings would be considered at the earliest possible opportunity, and should not be delayed where it is necessary.[260]

PD16A indicates, inter alia, that:

a. Making the child a party to the proceedings is a step that will be taken only in cases which involve an issue of significant difficulty and consequently will occur in only a minority of cases.[261]

b. Before taking the decision to make the child a party, consideration should be given to alternative preferable routes, such as asking a Cafcass officer to carry out further work, or by making a referral to social services, or possibly by obtaining expert evidence.[262]

c. The decision to make the child a party will always be exclusively that of the court.[263]

d. It must be recognised that separate representation of the child may result in a delay in the resolution of the proceedings. When deciding whether to direct that a child be made a party, the court will take into account the risk of delay or other facts adverse to the welfare of the child.[264]

---

[260] *Re A (Children) (Parental alienation)* [2019] 9 WLUK 445, para. 13(x)

[261] PD16A, para. 7.1

[262] PD16A, para. 7.1

[263] PD16A, para. 7.2

[264] PD16A, para. 7.3

e. The court's primary consideration will be the best interests of the child.

It is clear from PD16A that the particular circumstances of the case will be relevant to the court's decision. The guidance list that is provided[265] is non-exhaustive, and notes that some compelling reasons for joining a child as a party to the proceedings include:

a. *where a (Cafcass) officer has notified the court that in the opinion of that officer the child should be made a party;*

b. *where the child has a standpoint or interest which is inconsistent with or incapable of being represented by any of the adult parties;*

c. *where there is an intractable dispute over residence or contact, including where all contact has ceased, or where there is irrational but implacable hostility to contact or where the child may be suffering harm associated with the contact dispute;*

d. *where the views and wishes of the child cannot be adequately met by a report to the court;*

e. *where an older child is opposing a proposed course of action;*

f. *where there are complex medical or mental health issues to be determined or there are other unusually complex issues that necessitate separate representation of the child;*

g. *where there are international complications outside child abduction, in particular where it may be necessary for there to be discussions with overseas authorities or a foreign court;*

h. *where there are serious allegations of physical, sexual or other abuse in relation to the child or there are allegations of domestic violence not capable of being resolved with the help of a* (Cafcass) *officer.*

[265] PD16A, para. 7.2

i. *where the proceedings concern more than one child and the welfare of the children is in conflict or one child is in a particularly disadvantaged position;*

j. *where there is a contested issue about scientific testing.*

Rule 16.4 guardians

When a child is joined to proceedings, the court will usually appoint a guardian to promote their welfare and best interests. In fact, pursuant to FPR 2010 r.16.4 there is in fact an obligation on the court to appoint a guardian for a child who is made a party pursuant to r.16.2.[266]

This in practice means that in most private children disputes in which it is deemed in the child's best interests to join them as a party to the proceedings, Cafcass will be invited to assign a r.16.4 guardian to the child. It is important to note that enquiries should be undertaken with Cafcass or Cafcass Cymru before appointing an officer to act as a child's guardian. Ideally, these will be undertaken by the representatives of the parties in advance of an application being made to join a child to proceedings, however the court is also able to make these enquiries.[267] If Cafcass or Cafcass Cymru are unable to provide a children's guardian without delay, pursuant to FPR 2010 r.16.24 the court is also able to appoint the Official Solicitor or a person other than the Official Solicitor if they consent to the appointment. This may involve the appointment of a guardian from the National Youth Advocacy Service ('NYAS'), for example, an organisation that Munby J (as he then was), in the case of *Re D (Intractable Contact Dispute: Publicity)*[268], expressly endorsed when discussing the separate representation of a child in cases of intractable contact:

> *"As Wall J pointed out in Re M at para [15], intractable contact disputes are one of the "prime categories" for separate representation of the children. I agree. I also agree that in this situation the court can with great advantage make use of organisations such as the National*

[266] FPR 2010, r.16.4(c)

[267] See PD16A, para. 7.4(a)

[268] [2004] EWHC 727 (Fam)

Youth Advisory Service (NYAS), an organisation whose assistance in A v A was justifiably lauded by Wall J (see at paras [24], [131]–[133])."[269]

An order appointing a children's guardian may be made by the court of its own initiative (on joining a child as party to proceedings, for example), or on the application of a person who wishes to be the children's guardian, or a party of the proceedings.[270]

Once appointed, the guardian thereon has a duty to fairly and competently conduct proceedings on behalf of the child, must have no interest in the proceedings adverse to the child, and must take all steps and decisions for the benefit of the child.[271]

Representation through a solicitor

Whilst it is most common when a child is joined to proceedings for the child to be represented through a guardian, in certain cases it may be appropriate to appoint a solicitor to represent the child directly. As discussed at length throughout this Chapter, the wishes and feelings of the child are often muddied by the influence of a parent in cases of parental alienation. As such, whilst joinder and separate representation of children may be considered, it is important to remember that such measures will be rare in cases involving findings or allegations of parental alienation.

In private law proceedings under the 1989 Act, a child may conduct proceedings without a children's guardian (or litigation friend), if:

a. the child has obtained the court's permission.[272] This includes circumstances the child already has a litigation friend or children's guardian, and wishes to conduct the remaining stages of proceedings without the litigation friend or the guardian. In such

[269] ibid., para. 51

[270] FPR, r.16.24(2)

[271] PD16A, para. 7.6

[272] FPR 2010, r.16.6(3)(a)

circumstances permission will need to be given by the court for the removal of the litigation friend or children's guardian.[273]

b. a solicitor considers that the child is able, having regard to the child's understanding, to give instructions in relation to the proceedings and has accepted instructions from that child to act for that child in the proceedings and, if the proceedings have begun, the solicitor is already acting.[274] The solicitor must inform the court immediately.[275]

In considering (a) above, the court will only give permission if it considers that "*the child has sufficient understanding to conduct the proceedings concerned without a litigation friend or children's guardian.*"[276]

It should be noted that even if permission if given however, the court may require that the litigation friend or children's guardian continue to continue to take part in the proceedings as the court directs.[277]

'Sufficient understanding'

The leading judgment of Black LJ in *Re W (A Child) (Public Law proceedings: child's separate representation)*[278] neatly encapsulates the evolution of the issue of separate representation of children, and in particular the meaning of 'sufficient understanding':

> *"26. I think it is fair to say that views about children's involvement in legal proceedings have continued to evolve since 2005. This is not the place for a comprehensive review of developments, and nor is one necessary because, in Re F (Children) [2016] EWCA Civ 546, which was decided after Judge Williams made her decision about FW's separate representation, the President of the Family Division (with whom Arden LJ agreed) set out the highlights of the jurisprudence,*

[273] FPR 2010, r. 16.6(5)

[274] FPR 2010, r.16.6(3)(b)

[275] FPR 2010, r.16.6(9)

[276] FPR 2010, r.16.6(6)

[277] FPR 2010, r.16.6(7)

[278] [2016] EWCA Civ 1051

starting at §35 of his judgment. By way of example, the evolutionary process has included developments in relation to children giving evidence in family proceedings (Re W (Children) (Family Proceedings: Evidence) [2010] UKSC 12, [2010] 1 FLR 1485), guidelines to encourage judges to enable children to feel more involved and connected with proceedings in which important decisions are made in their lives (Guidelines for Judges Meeting Children who are Subject to Family Proceedings [2010] 2 FLR 1872), the involvement of the Children and Vulnerable Witnesses Working Group (culminating in a final report dated February 2015, see [2015] Family Law 443), and recognition that the child's state of mind may have a part to play in establishing habitual residence (Re LC (Children) [2014] UKSC 1). Summing the position up at §41 of his judgment, the President said:

> *"It is apparent that in relation to all these matters there has been a sea-change in attitudes over the last decade and more, even if on occasion practitioners and the courts have been and still are too slow to recognise the need for change or to acknowledge the pace of change. Moreover, and I wish to emphasise this, the process of change continues apace."*

27. The question of whether a child is able, having regard to his or her understanding, to instruct a solicitor must be approached having in mind this acknowledgement of the autonomy of children and of the fact that it can at times be in their interests to play some direct part in the litigation about them. What is sufficient understanding in any given case will depend upon all the facts. In this particular case, in my judgment, the criticisms made by Ms Giz of Her Honour Judge Williams' approach, taken together, fatally undermine the decision that she took. The careful submissions on behalf of the local authority and the guardian in support of her determination failed to persuade me otherwise. [...]

36. Sometimes there will be a clear answer to the question whether the child is able, having regard to his or her understanding, to give their own instructions to a solicitor. In cases of more difficulty, the court will have to take a down to earth approach to determining the issue, avoiding too sophisticated an examination of the position and recognising that it is unlikely to be desirable (or even possible) to attempt to assemble definitive evidence about the matter at this stage of the proceedings. All will depend upon the individual circumstances of the case and it is impossible to provide a route map to the solution. However, it is worth noting particularly that, given the public funding problems, the judge will have to be sure to take whatever steps are possible to ensure that the child's point of view in relation to separate representation is sufficiently before the court. The judge will expect to be guided by the guardian and by those solicitors who have formed a view as to whether they could accept instructions from the child. Then it will be for the judge to form his or her own view on the material available at that stage in the proceedings, sometimes (but certainly not always) including expert opinion on the question of understanding (see Re H (A Minor) (Care Proceedings: Child's Wishes) [1993] 1 FLR 440, at 450). Understanding can be affected by all sorts of things, including the age of the child, his or her intelligence, his or her emotional and/or psychological and/or psychiatric and/or physical state, language ability, influence etc. The child will obviously need to comprehend enough of what the case is about (without being expected to display too sophisticated an understanding) and must have the capacity to give his or her own coherent instructions, without being more than usually inconsistent. If the judge requires an expert report to assist in determining the question of understanding, the child should be under no illusions about the importance of keeping the appointment with the expert concerned. It is an opportunity for the child to demonstrate that he or she does have the necessary understanding and there is always a risk that a failure to attend will be taken to show a failure to understand."

Black LJ identified particular issues giving rise to difficulties in the evolution of understanding as including:

i. The risk of placing too much weight in the evaluation of the child's understanding of allegations of influence or manipulation of the child by a parent.

ii. The fact that a child's views may be considered to be misguided does not necessarily mean the child does not have sufficient understanding to instruct a solicitor.

iii. The danger of the court becoming too embroiled in consideration of i) and ii) above such that it pre-judges what may be central issues in the substantive application.

iv. The need to balance the harm that might be caused by direct participation with the harm that might be caused by refusal of direct participation.

LJ Black's summary as outlined above was given express endorsement by Williams J in of *CS v SBH & Ors.*[279] The case involved a twelve-year-old child's appeal concerning the variation of a lives with order. In evaluating whether the child had 'sufficient understanding' to conduct the proceedings, the court considered that there had been a "*shift away from a paternalistic approach in favour of an approach which gave significantly more weight to the autonomy of the child.*"[280] Thus, the earlier authorities (considered extensively in the judgment) had to be approached with a degree of caution in terms of the level at which they set the "bar" of understanding. Williams J notes:

> *"i) In assessing understanding the court is likely to attribute more weight to the child's views of the issues and the reasons they give for wishing to be involved amongst others. The expression of a wish for an objectively 'unwise' (or unsound) outcome might now not undermine the evaluation of sufficient understanding in the way it might have in 1993. It is perhaps also likely to hold the child to a somewhat lower expectation of understanding of the litigation process than emerges from Booth J's judgment cited in Re N (above) which appeared to contemplate an ability to negotiate complexities of litigation which many adults might struggle with.*
>
> *ii) In so far as the welfare of the child is a primary consideration in the decision-making process (Art 3 UNCRC and Mabon suggest it is) the welfare of the child sounds both in favour of their involvement (recognising the value they may add to the process and their rights as a*

[279] [2019] EWHC 634 (Fam)

[280] ibid., para 63

person significantly affected by the decision) and against (where involvement may expose them to harmful emotional consequences)."[281]

Williams J considered that the relevant factors when determining whether the child has sufficient understanding, and summarised them as follows[282]:

i. *"The level of intelligence of the child.*

ii. *The emotional maturity of the child.*

iii. *Factors which might undermine their understanding such as issues arising from their emotional, psychological, psychiatric or emotional state.*

iv. *Their reasons for wishing to instruct a solicitor directly or to act without a guardian and the strength of feeling accompanying the wish to play a direct role.*

v. *Their understanding of the issues in the case and their desired outcome, any matter which sheds light on the extent to which those are authentically their own or are mere parroting of one parents position. Some degree of influence is a natural component of decision making but the closer to the 'parroting' end of the spectrum one gets the lower the level of understanding there is likely to be. An unwise decision does not mean the child does not understand although it will no doubt depend on the extent to which the child's view diverges from an objectively reasonable or wise decision.*

vi. *Their understanding of the process of litigation including the function of their lawyer, the role of the judge, the role they might play and the law that is applied and some of the consequences of involvement in litigation. Care should be taken not to impose too high a level of understanding in this regard; many adults with capacity would not and we should not expect it from children. An ability to understand that their solicitor put their case but also has duties of honesty to the*

[281] ibid., para. 63

[282] ibid., para. 64

court, an ability to understand that the judge makes a decision based on an overall evaluation of the best interests of the child which balances many competing factors; the ability to understand that they might attend court, could give and evidence, could read documents; the ability to recognise the stress of exposure to the court process and the arguments between others. The presence of all of these would be powerful signs of a high level of understanding. Conversely the absence of them or evidence of a distorted understanding would be contra-indicators.

vii. The court's assessment of the risk of harm to the child of direct participation for the risk of harm arising from excluding the child from direct participation and the child's appreciation of the risks of harm."

Ultimately, joinder of a child to proceedings and separate representation might be a useful tool available to the court in cases when other methods of ascertaining the child's wishes and feelings have been unsuccessful. Consideration must be given to joinder as early as possible in the process as the court will always be concerned about the impact of delay. A degree of caution must be adopted however to ensure that a child is not joined prematurely and in advance of determining the factual matrix, in particular if it is to be the case that the child is to be represented directly through a solicitor, and without a guardian. In such circumstances it will be difficult to assess the child's understanding, and the repercussions of the child instructing legal representation of their own in circumstances where they are merely a conduit of one of the parents' views can be self-defeating and cut against the purposes for joinder in the first place.

CHAPTER SEVEN

TRANSFERS OF RESIDENCE

The legal position

Terminology

A transfer of residence is the term of art used for a type of child arrangement order which transfers with whom the child lives from one parent to the other. In the context of cases involving allegations of parental alienation, this is most frequently a transfer from the resident, alienating parent to the non-resident, alienated parent. It can however be a transfer to a third party, such as grandparents or other family members.

Child arrangement orders were introduced in April 2014 by the CFA 2014. They replace contact orders and residence orders. Section 8 of the 1989 Act provides the court with the power to make a child arrangements order which is defined as an order regulating arrangements relating to:

a. *With whom* a child is to live, spend time or otherwise have contact, and

b. *When* a child is to live, spend time or otherwise have contact with any person.

Whilst the phrase 'transfer of residence' is used throughout this Chapter and in a number of decisions post-April 2014 as something of a shorthand, to do so is in no way intended to diminish the importance of the replacement of residence orders with child arrangement orders. Alternative phraseology could be transfer of living arrangements.

A judicial weapon of last resort?

The law in respect of transfers of a child's residence has undergone significant change over the last decade. Nonetheless it remains important to consider the legal framework historically applied in order to understand the court's revised approach.

For a number of years the court treated a transfer of residence as a last resort. As summarised by Coleridge J in the decision of *Re A (Residence Order)*[283]:

> "[...] *These cases are the scourge of the whole family justice system and are always extremely difficult to resolve. They do indeed demand a robust response from all of us involved in the system. The remedy of transferring residence from one parent to the non-resident parent is an essential weapon or tool in these cases as a weapon or tool of last resort. It may indeed be a case of putting a gun to a parent's head to force her or him to rethink, as counsel described it, but that, it seems to me, is a legitimate approach and remedy. However, whereas here there has been an apparent volte-face by a mother and a concession that now contact should happen, combined with an acceptance by all that the mother's care was in all other respects adequate, the remedy of last resort needs to be deployed with great care and any apparent change of heart, it seems to me, fully tested.*"[284]

Similar wording was used by Thorpe LJ in his judgment in the same case. Thorpe LJ considered an order to transfer residence as an order that by its nature is a *"draconian"* step, and said as follows:

> *"The transfer of residence from the obdurate primary carer to the parent frustrated in pursuit of contact is a judicial weapon of last resort. There was hardly a need for a psychologist to establish the risks of moving these girls from mother to father, not only after her long years of care but also in the light of the negative picture that they had been given of a father who they had not effectively seen for 17 months. The risks of gamesmanship from the mother in the future, confirmed in residence but nailed down with a clear detailed contact order, were plainly less, and from that essential risk balance the judge was diverted.*

283 [2009] EWCA Civ 1141

284 ibid., at para. 21

In a sense it could be said that the order she made was premature and in its draconian content too risky for these children."[285]

The current approach

The current position has been summarised by Sir Andrew McFarlane PFD in the decision of *Re L (A Child)*.[286] Sir Andrew McFarlane PFD makes the following remarks in respect of the use of terminology such as "*a weapon*" or "*a tool*" in *Re A (Residence Order)*:

> "[...] *I would wish to distance myself from the language used insofar as it refers to a decision to change residence of a child as being "a weapon" or "a tool". Whilst such language may be apt in discussion between one lawyer and another in the context of consideration of the forensic options available to a judge who is seeking to move a case on, such language, in my view, risks moving the focus of the decision-making away from the welfare of the child which must be the court's paramount consideration."*[287]

Sir Andrew McFarlane PFD continues to emphasise that the child's welfare is paramount when making any decision as to whether to transfer the residence of a child. In particular, a warning is given in respect of the dangers of putting any gloss upon the paramountcy principle section 1 of the 1989 Act with phraseology such as "*last resort*" or "*draconian*", and the suggestion that there is an *"enhanced welfare test"* in decisions involving a potential transfer of residence:

> *"Having considered the authorities to which I have referred, and others, there is, in my view, a danger in placing too much emphasis on the phrase "last resort" used by Thorpe LJ and Coleridge J in Re: A. It is well established that the court cannot put a gloss on to the paramountcy principle in CA 1989, s 1. I do not read the judgments in Re: A as purporting to do that. The test is, and must always be, based on a comprehensive analysis of the child's welfare and a*

---

[285] ibid., para. 18. Coleridge J also referred to the transfer of residence order in such terms in *Re A (Suspended Residence Order)* [2009] EWHC 1576, para. 15

[286] [2019] EWHC 867 (Fam),

[287] ibid., para. 54

determination of where the welfare balance points in terms of outcome. It is important to note that the welfare provisions in CA 1989, s 1 are precisely the same provisions as those applying in public law children cases where a local authority may seek the court's authorisation to remove a child from parental care either to place them with another relative or in alternative care arrangements. Where, in private law proceedings, the choice, as here, is between care by one parent and care by another parent against whom there are no significant findings, one might anticipate that the threshold triggering a change of residence would, if anything, be lower than that justifying the permanent removal of a child from a family into foster care. Use of phrases such as "last resort" or "draconian" cannot and should not indicate a different or enhanced welfare test. What is required is for the judge to consider all the circumstances in the case that are relevant to the issue of welfare, consider those elements in the s 1(3) welfare check list which apply on the facts of the case and then, taking all those matters into account, determine which of the various options best meets the child's welfare needs."[288]

The holistic welfare exercise in transfer of residence cases

In *Re F (A Child) (Internal Relocation Cases)*[289], Ryder LJ confirmed that the holistic welfare balancing exercise applies just as much to private law cases as it does to public law cases (see **Chapter 2: General principles regarding contact**).

The holistic welfare exercise in all cases in which there are allegations of parental alienation involves some degree of weighing up the short-term consequences of a child objecting to contact as against the long-term benefits of a relationship with the alienated parent. Whilst Judges are encouraged to take a medium to long-term view and not accord excessive weight to short-term and transient problems in establishing contact between a child and the non-resident parent,[290] when considering whether a transfer of residence is the appropriate solution, the child's response in the short-term to a move is often an important consideration

---

288 ibid., para. 59

289 [2015] EWCA Civ 882

290 *Re C (A Child)* [2011] EWCA Civ 521, para. 47

in the welfare balancing exercise. A transfer of residence will nearly always be made against both the resident parent and the child's wishes, albeit the degree of objection will vary. Therefore, in most cases involving a transfer of residence there will be a consideration of the balance of harm; the harm resulting from the child remaining with the alienating parent and being denied a relationship with the other parent, as against the harm that may be caused in effecting a move, including the risk of trauma if the change of primary carer is not handled sensitively.

The likely impact on a child of any change in residence from one parent to the other is something professionals may have assessed within the course of proceedings.[291] The manner in which the child historically responded to contact; the extent of the child's objections to a transfer of residence; the child's age, and (often crucially) the degree to which the move is supported or undermined by the resident parent; are just some factors which may indicate a child's likely response.

Alongside the harm that could potentially be caused to a child through effecting a transfer of residence, the court will also be considering ways to minimise that harm, and the risk of a transfer of residence going wrong. Sometimes this consideration will sit alongside the welfare exercise. The court may determine that a mitigating factor can reduce the likelihood of a child reacting in a certain way, in turn minimising the likely degree of harm of effecting a move. Alternatively, the court may determine that no mitigating factors can adequately safeguard the child against the risks. In nearly all cases however, once a decision has been reached that it is in a child's welfare interests to transfer residence, as a subsequent step the court will turn its mind to designing a robust and bespoke process with which to effect that change (see below).

Example cases

The below cases represent a selection of example decisions from the last two decades. Most of them in which either a finding of alienation or

[291] For an extensive and thorough example of the sort of balancing exercise that may be undertaken by professionals in advising the court, see the summary or the expert opinion provided by Coleridge J in the decision of *Re A (Suspended Residence Order)* [2009] EWHC 1576 (Fam) at paras. 67-89

implacable hostility had been made, and in which it was determined that a transfer of residence was in the child(ren)'s welfare interests.

- In *V v V (Children) (Contact: Implacable Hostility)*[292], Bracewell J acceded to the father's application for a residence order in respect of his two daughters aged seven and nine. The mother had made false and exaggerated allegations against the father and paternal family in order to frustrate contact and had coached the children. It was found that she had subjected them to emotional abuse in the form of unnecessary interviews with the police and visits to the hospital. Remaining with the mother would likely subject them to further emotional harm, and while attaching a penal notice to the contact order may mean contact is more likely to take place, it would not stop the mother poisoning the children's minds. The children's need to have a relationship with their father could only therefore be met by transferring residence to him.

- In *Re A (A Child) (Change of Residence)*[293] the Court of Appeal held that the Recorder at first instance had been entitled to order a transfer of residence in circumstances where this had been the firm recommendation of a psychologist and independent social worker. The mother had been assessed as having a personality disorder and had continually interrupted and interfered with the father's contact despite numerous warnings. It was concluded that the short-term trauma that may be suffered by a change in residence would likely be outweighed by the long-term benefits. The Court of Appeal cautioned however that in refusing to stay the execution of the transfer of residence, which was ordered to take place over the weekend immediately after the judgment, despite an indication of by the mother of an intention to appeal, may have eroded the facility for an effective appeal. While the result would have likely been the same, consideration needed to be given to making an order which afforded the aspiring appellant a narrow opportunity to approach the court for further, temporary, relief before the order took effect, subject of course to the welfare of the child remaining

[292] [2004] EWHC 1215 (Fam)

[293] [2007] EWCA Civ 899

paramount. The result in this case would likely have been the same however (a dismissal of the appeal).

- In *Re W (Residence: Leave to Appeal),*[294] the Court of Appeal refused permission for a mother to appeal an order transferring residence to the father of the parties' daughter. The mother had falsely claimed the father was not their daughter's father, had made unsubstantiated allegations he had committed acts of domestic violence, was a paedophile, was selling drugs, and had a blood infection that would infect the child. Out of the thirty-four contact visits that had been ordered, only two had gone ahead with the mother failing to take the child to twenty-nine of them without proper reason. The court made clear that *if* the judge had been transferring residence as a means of punishing the mother for failing to obey court orders, this would have been an inappropriate exercise of discretion. However, the judge had taken the view that the child's long-term welfare required a transfer given she was likely to suffer significant harm if she remained in her mother's care. The mother's appeal had no reasonable prospects of success.

- In *Re V (A Child),*[295] the Court of Appeal held that the judge at first instance had been entitled to transfer residence from the mother to the father where the mother had allegedly inculcated false memories in the child that she had been physically and sexually assaulted by her father. While a change in residence would be traumatic it would be more harmful for the child to remain exposed to the distorted memories that the mother was fabricating. The judge had been entitled to place weight on this pivotal factor that outweighed all others in the welfare balancing exercise.

- In *Re L (A Child),*[296] the Court of Appeal concluded that the trial Judge had been entitled to transfer the residence of a six-year-old child from his mother to his father. There was no factual basis for the other's antagonistic approach to the father. She had ignored

---

294 [2010] EWCA Civ 1280

295 [2013] EWCA Civ 1649

296 [2014] EWCA Civ 167

contact orders, changed the child's address twice without informing the father or the courts and had to be traced. Temporary residence was granted over Easter 2013 after the mother failed to attend the interim hearing. In making the change of residence final, the judge had not erred. It was triggered by the mother's conduct over a long period, and the mother had been warned on multiple occasions about the court's powers and knew that the transfer of residence may become substantive.

- In *Re H (A Child) (Parental Alienation),*[297] Keehan J transferred the residence of a child from his mother to father after findings of alienation had been made. Keehan J concluded that trauma and harm that would be suffered as a result of being transferred to the father's care, and the potential for adverse consequences, was outweighed by the fact a transfer was the only means by which the child would be able to enjoy a relationship with both parents. An expert in the field of parental alienation, Dr Janine Braier (psychiatrist), had produced a report in this case which concluded the mother had alienated the child; the child was likely to continue suffering significant social harm with the current arrangements, and it was very likely that if the child remained with mother, he would not enjoy any sort of a relationship with his father. A transfer of residence was recommended as the only feasible route. This was a case in which the expert evidence before the court in respect of the child's presentation and responses was decisive in the Judge concluding alienation had occurred.

- In *Re T (Parental Alienation)*[298] Judge Raeside QC concluded it was in a five-year-old child's best interests to transfer her care from her mother to her father. Numerous findings had been made including that the child had suffered, and continued to suffer, emotional harm from living with her mother, denying her a positive paternal relationship and presenting an extremely negative picture of the father to her daughter. While not underestimating the difficulty for this child of moving to her father from her

[297] [2019] EWHC 2723 (Fam)

[298] [2019] EWHC 3854 (Fam)

primary carer, and the fact she would undoubtedly struggle in the short-term and be confused and upset by the change, the Judge concluded she would not find it traumatising if handled sensitively. The child's emotional needs were not being met by the mother, who was incapable of meeting them, and the harm she would continue to suffer of being denied a relationship with her father outweighed this risk.

- In *Re A and B (Parental Alienation: No. 1)*[299], the first of four judgments in a case concerning two children aged fourteen and eleven, the court transferred residence from the mother to the father in circumstances where two of the experts in the case, Dr Janine Braier (psychiatrist) and Karen Woodall (psychotherapist), who had worked collaboratively with the family for a period of fifteen-months, had been unsuccessful in implementing a 50/50 shared care arrangement. The court heard extensive evidence from the experts in the case (see **Chapter 5: Options available for the court**), in particular in respect of the merits of further therapeutic work and the potential adverse consequences for both children if they continued to suffer parental alienation and splitting from the father. The court balanced the five options that were being considered by the experts as potential solutions to the problem, which ranged from a full transfer to the father's care with only supervised contact with the mother, varying shared care arrangements (80/20; 70/30 or 65/35), and the present 50/50 shared care arrangement. Keehan J concluded as follows:

  "52. I do not consider that any of these options meet the welfare best interests of the children. I have already explained why I consider the present 50/50 shared care is neither in the welfare best interests of the children nor sustainable. I acknowledge that it is agreed that if the children were asked for their views, it is likely they would prefer the current 50/50 shared care arrangement to continue. It has to be borne in mind, however, that although the children love their mother and are aligned with her:

[299] [2020] EWHC 3366 (Fam)

(a) She has caused and is causing them emotional and psychological harm by alienating or splitting the children from their father; and

(b) They remain vulnerable to her changes of mood and behaviour most especially Child A.

53. I accept that all of the five options carry risks of one sort or another for the children. The risks which concern me the greatest are that:

(a) Child A and/or Child B will once again be alienated or split from their father with the consequence that it will not then be possible to repair the relationship between them; and/or

(b) The adverse consequences of their alienation from their father would render one or both of them beyond the control of either parent and/or results in the decision that one or both of them in their welfare best interests be placed in foster care.

I agree with Dr Braier that such an outcome would be a disaster for these bright and intelligent children.

54. I therefore have to find a solution to this family's crisis which seeks to achieve a balance between the following competing factors:

(a) One or other of the children rejecting the very limited contact with their mother and voting with their feet and leaving their father's care and/or disengaging with him; and

(b) Contact with the mother taking place at such a frequency and for such a prolonged period that the mother's malign influence results in the children being once again alienated or split from their father."

An order was made that the children live with their father.

- In *FA v MA*,[300] Judge Whybrow in the Family Court transferred the residence of a four-year-old child from her mother to father following the mother's persistent breaches of contact orders over several years. The mother had continued to make unilateral decisions without reference to the court, including taking the child out of the country and failing to surrender her and the child's passports when directed to do so. She had ignored the final hearing and made no proposals for the future for the child's relationship with her father. The judgment is a useful example of the court balancing a number of possible welfare options: video and postal contact; staying contact with the father; an order to be placed into foster care pending a move to the father; staying contact backed by a suspended transfer of residence order, and an immediate transfer of residence order. The court concluded suspending the transfer of residence order would likely delay the inevitable, and made an immediate transfer. While acknowledging it would cause distress and confusion in the immediate, in the medium to long-term it would provide the best opportunity for the child to have a meaningful relationship with both sides of her family.

- In *Re A and B (Child Arrangements: Parental Alienation)*,[301] Recorder Moys ordered the transfer of two children from their father to their mother in circumstances where findings had been made that he had deliberately tried to erode her from their lives, and they had suffered significant emotional harm. The father had unilaterally removed the children to Australia without the mother's consent. He was in breach of an interim order requiring him to return the children from Australia, and summary return proceedings were concurrently proceeding pursuant to the mother's application under the 1980 Hague Convention. The court made clear however that the transfer of residence order was not to be implemented until the court has approved a transition plan due to concerns about how they would emotionally cope with the change. The parents were prohibited, under a prohibited steps order with a penal notice, from communicating the decision to the

[300] [2021] EWFC 58

[301] [2022] 1 WLUK 440

children until a course of action had been approved and the clinical psychologist had advised how best to communicate the decision to them.

Interim transfers of residence

In certain cases, the court can take the unusual step of transferring residence at an interim stage. This may be particularly appropriate in circumstances in which there are mounting concerns about a parent's behaviour. This will most commonly happen in cases where there has been a fact-finding hearing at which the factual matrix has been determined, and a final welfare hearing has been listed separately thereafter.

In *Re Y (Private Law: Interim Change of Residence),*[302] Pauffley J transferred the child's residence post-fact-finding hearing and prior to the final hearing which was scheduled in just six weeks' time. The court did so owing to mounting and immediate concerns about the mother's "*fixed, unshakeable, persistent and enduring belief that Y has been sexually abused by her father*"[303], which was determined during the fact-finding hearing to be entirely without foundation.[304] The local authority had become increasingly concerned about the mother's mental state, obsessional anxiety and emotional unavailability to the child. The position of the local authority, supported by the guardian, was that continued placement with the mother was neither sustainable nor conductive to the child's wellbeing if unsupervised contact between her and the father was to take place as intended by the court. The mother objected to unsupervised contact and made clear she did not accept the findings of the court. Further, the child had sustained a number of largely unexplained injuries and physical symptoms, particularly bruises to her buttocks and close to her genital area sufficient to cause the local authority to initiate a section 47 investigation with an associated child protection medical. The mother had drawn a number of these to the social worker's attention, and plainly suggested they were caused by the

[302] [2014] EWHC 1068 (Fam)

[303] ibid., para. 11. See for a further description of some of the case recordings from the local authority.

[304] See *Re Y (A Child) (Private Law: Fact Finding)* [2014] EWHC 486 (Fam)

father despite professional opinion that the overwhelming likelihood was that there was no link between the bruises and any sinister sexual interference by the father.

Pauffley J noted:

> *"14.* [...] *the mother* [...] *has repeatedly demonstrated, in the clearest way possible, that she simply cannot meet an important element of Y's emotional need. She has no ability, currently, to accept that the father has done no harm to Y, sexually or otherwise. The mother's response to the father and the risk she has convinced herself he poses can only be profoundly unhealthy.*
>
> *15. Dr Asen's view as to the mother's beliefs is that they have an almost delusional quality. His fear was that sooner rather than later the mother would make further allegations of sexual abuse or misconduct against the father after unsupervised contact. Subsequent events have proved that forecast to be entirely accurate.*
>
> *16. I remain convinced that the mother's beliefs are entirely without foundation. They would seem to me to be the product of distorted thinking and to have their origins in the mother's own psychological problems. Her strong opposition to the father and to the role he should properly be playing in Y's life are based upon beliefs which do not connect with reality. They are intensely problematic from Y's perspective. The chances of her being able to make healthy progress in her relationship with her father would be severely limited if she were to continue to be exposed daily to the mother's beliefs and the florid manifestations of her own distress."*

In making an order transferring residence in the interim, Pauffley J noted:

> *"In so concluding I bear in mind all of those positive factors emphasised by Miss Jones and by the mother herself. Until now it is of course the reality that Y has always lived with her mother and L. In other areas of her development she is doing well. But the risks that she will never be able to consolidate a proper relationship with her father, as the result of her mother's overt and also her subtle attempts to undermine that*

> *relationship are so great, so transparently obvious, that the father should now have an interim residence order."*[305]

Nonetheless, the importance of not transferring residence prematurely, and in advance of a full understanding of the factual matrix, has been emphasised by Williams J in the recent case of *Re M (Children) (Interim Change of Residence).*[306] In this case, the father sought an immediate transfer of the children's residence to his care on an urgent basis. For a number of reasons the parties had agreed in adopting a therapeutic approach with a family therapist, and a fact-finding route had not been pursued. However, matters deteriorated and the family therapist was soon recommending a transfer of the children into the father's care. Williams J noted the following in respect of interim decisions of this nature:

> *"18. […] I entirely accept the Court can act by transferring residence on an interim basis. The Court is often called upon to consider interim placement decisions in urgent circumstances and without the opportunity and time to gather all the evidence that would be available for a final or a fact-finding hearing. In my experience such considerations tend to arise where there is a clear safeguarding issue that must be confronted* ***there and then*** *and where to delay would leave the children at risk of harm. Nonetheless in such cases the Court must act with caution given the potentially profound impact on a child of such a move. The Court must also be astute to the possibility that 'first appearances' are not necessary 'last appearances' and that many cases take significant changes of direction as the evidence is gathered and then carefully examined. My judgment is that interim decisions shifting residence can, and sometimes must be made but the arguments underlaying the proposal must always be considered with robust scrutiny and a transfer should typically not be granted where the case appears unclear or finely balanced. In such circumstances it is likely to be better for the 'fog to clear' or the evidence to be fuller before reaching a decision on the application. For the avoidance of doubt this logic is*

---

305 *Re Y (Private Law: Interim Change of Residence)* [2014] EWHC 1068 (Fam)., para. 22

306 [2020] 12 WLUK 685

entirely consistent with the welfare of the child as paramount factor as it is placing particular regard to 'the likely effect on the child of a change in circumstances'. In considering applications for change of residence I also accept that the language of 'change of residence as last resort' is an inappropriate gloss on the paramountcy principle.

19. I accept fact finding is not required prior to an interim decision or change of residence. By way of an example only, a Court may order interim transfer where a child suffers serious physical harm in the care of the other parent and the surrounding circumstances remain unclear. The factual matrix may not be agreed but the Court may be required to elevate safeguarding over the risk of a child being moved from a safe carer. [...] However, there will be cases where fact-finding is a pre-requisite before approving a change of residence. Each case will turn on its facts as to the relevance and necessity of fact-finding whether at an interim stage or later within the proceedings. In many cases where alienation is alleged the Court has to properly examine the circumstances of the case to ensure a welfare focused decision has been reached. Too often one parent's allegation of alienation is met by the other parent's reference to inappropriate conduct on the part of the applying parent (and often vis a vis). The Court has experience of both alienating conduct but also estrangements that derives directly from the actions of the applying parent. In the latter case in my judgment it would be contrary to the welfare of the child to enact an interim transfer into the care of the applying parent where the underlying circumstances had not been properly considered and the move itself might therefore cause harm to the child."

In this case, Williams J concluded a transfer to be premature due to the unresolved factual matrix and uncertainties in respect of the underlying family dynamic. No attempts had been made to ascertain the children's views on such a transfer, and closer scrutiny was required as to why their relationship with their father had fractured. There were a number of additional features which had the potential to shape or influence the children's views, separate from the mother's role, including but not limited to the mother's allegations in respect of the family's experience in an abusive religious sect; one of the children's concerns about her father's behaviour towards her, including stripping and showering her with cold water, and the impact of the father's parenting more generally.[307] Without sufficiently analysing the veracity and impact of all of this, Williams J concluded it unwise to reach settled conclusions as to alienation as the cause, and too premature to effect such a significant and experimental change of residence.[308]

Suspended transfers of residence

The court is also able to order a suspended transfer of residence. Such an order makes the transfer dependent upon compliance by the alienating parent with clearly defined terms in the child arrangements order. This may, in the right case, have the effect of ensuring the alienating parent acquiesces to any child arrangements order for contact between the child and non-resident parent, and promotes the arrangements that have been endorsed by the court. The result of not doing so will be for the suspension of the transfer of residence to be lifted and the order enforced. It is a 'last chance saloon' for the alienating parent before the court resorts to more drastic action.

An example of a decision in which such an approach was adopted is *Re A (Suspended Residence Order).*[309] The father and paternal grandparents in this case had applied for an immediate transfer of the parties' two sons to the paternal grandparents' care, with a view to gradually re-introducing them to the father. In this case, the parties' two children lived with the mother. Significant allegations of serious sexual abuse had been made by the mother's daughter from a previous relationship against the father. Whilst these allegations were in fact substantiated, the court concluded that the father had not abused either of his sons. The mother refused to accept this finding – direct contact orders were repeatedly and deliberately breached, and the boys had not seen their father for three-and-a-half years. While she had on third day of the final hearing, after hearing the evidence of experts, allowed some contact to take place, within a month of that hearing she had decided there would be no further contact, including inexplicably with the paternal grandparents. This remained her position at the time of the hearing in which the court was

---

307 ibid. para. 31

308 See ibid. para. 53 for a summary of Williams J's conclusions.

309 [2009] EWHC 1576 (Fam)

considering a transfer of residence. It was concluded that the children had suffered significant emotional harm as a result of the mother demonising both the father and the paternal grandparents, including promoting in at least one of the children the false belief that he had been abused. They did not wish to have anything to do with their father or grandparents. As the mother had shown no sign she was willing or able to change her view or desist in her false belief that they had been abused, the court concluded that the only option was a transfer of residence to the paternal grandparents. In balancing the emotional trauma of a move from their primary carer in the short-term against the damage that would be caused by the mother's actions, Coleridge J remarked:

> "[...] *Without doubt a move would be very painful especially in the short term. It would also be harmful, in the longer term, to disrupt their primary attachment to their mother. But would it be as harmful, in the long term, as their being continually and unrelentingly exposed to their mother's false beliefs combined with her unremitting hostility to the paternal family undiluted by contact to them? In the end I do not think so.*"[310]

The residence order was not however to take effect immediately but to be suspended on the condition that the mother complied with a new contact order. If she did not do so fully, the suspension would be lifted immediately, and the children transferred to the paternal grandparents as soon as practicable. The court, in considering this issue, concluded:

> "*123.* [...] *the question still arises as to the date from when such an order might be brought into effect given what I have said about the best solution in para [116] above. Should the order be suspended in its effect to admit of the slim possibility that the mother will see the sense in not making the children change their whole lives in support of her campaign to exclude the D's from their lives when, if she was to remain intransigent, it would in fact, achieve the opposite result ?*
>
> *124. Both the father and grandparents oppose it. They both maintain that this will merely lead to further delay when the move to the grandparents is in reality inevitable. Things have gone too far and*

[310] ibid., para. 118

reached such a pitch that only immediate transfer is in the children's interests. They point especially to the recent letters.[311]

125. It seems to me (and the experts) that this 'suspended' course has one very clear advantage; the future residence of the children depends entirely on the mother's and to a lesser extent, the children's decision and action. If she (and they) abide by the court order the children stay with her (with all the obvious advantages). If she ignores it, the suspension on the order will be lifted immediately and the children move to make their home with the grandparents with all that that entails for their life. It is her choice and to a lesser extent their choice. But it is really entirely up to her.

126. I have decided it is the best way forward. If the boys stay put but the mother's influence is mitigated by regular and proper contact it would still be the best course."

A note of caution: this approach does not always work and can simply delay the inevitable. In some circumstances, a suspended transfer of residence is simply not enough to effect a change in approach from the alienating parent. In *Re S (Parental Alienation: Cult)*[312], the Court of Appeal considered and upheld a trial Judge's (HHJ Meston) finding that parental alienation had started to occur, particularly because of the influence of the mother's adherence to the activities and teachings cult of Universal Medicine, and the child's feelings that the father was different because he did not follow her and her mother's belief. The court had considered the evidence put forward by the father in respect of the cult of Universal Medicine, and concluded that it has some potentially

---

[311] The mother's most recent letter to the court had stated: "*JA's* [the father's] *parental rights need to be permanently removed and he should not be able to live a free life and therefore destroy the lives of others. He should especially not be able to come into contact with any children and should be locked away and removed from society for the safety of others. Even if extreme measures were to be taken: castration, or having a section of his brain removed (as is practised in certain states in America) who knows if JA could ever truly change. I would not want him as my next door neighbour had I not known him and if justice were to be served, allowing the public to know the truth then no one would ...*" Coleridge J regarded this as "*very worrying insight into the mother's current somewhat wild frame of mind,*" para. 62

[312] [2020] EWCA Civ 568

harmful and sinister elements, including a 2018 decision from the Supreme Court of New South Wales which concluded it was a socially harmful cult and its founder (Serge Benhayon) was a sexual predator who assaulted female students and had an indecent interest in children. There was evidence the child's diet was being restricted, the child was making comments praising Serge Benhayon and denigrating the father, and demonstrating peculiar behaviours.

The independent social worker, Helena Ware, stated that the mother had not understood the gravity of the concerns about Universal Medicine. She described the mother as "*deeply steeped in the teachings including restricted diet, sleep patterns, esoteric massages and the spiritual aspects of The Way of Livingness.*"[313] The independent social worker concluded that if she continued to be associated with it she would influence the child, who was also at risk of being alienated from her father and suffering harm. It was doubtful that she could extricate herself without significant therapeutic support and genuine commitment to doing so. Unless she did so, a transfer of residence was recommended.

HHJ Meston concluded that the child would find it upsetting if her time with the mother was curtailed, and considered that the mother's desire to do all that was reasonably required of her, including not engaging with Universal Medicine and giving appropriate undertakings, was sincere and genuine.

The Court of Appeal, whilst refusing to interfere with HHJ Meston's findings of fact, including that alienation had started to occur and the child was at risk of harm as a result of the mother's belief, held there were errors in his evaluation and balancing of the risks. It was unclear why the trial Judge thought the mother was likely to modify her thinking about Universal Medicine and Serge Benhayon – she had not even read the Australian court's decision, and made no true commitment to dissociate herself from the cult or engage in substantial therapy to do so. She had also refused to give sufficient undertakings. The Court of Appeal concluded that the Judge, having made findings of alienation, should have also taken effective steps to address it. HHJ Meston had not

[313] ibid., para. 41

balanced the various risk factors sufficiently or contrasted the long-term harm from Universal Medicine and parental alienation with the short-to-medium term harm caused by a move: *"In our view, that minimised the continuing and untreated harm to Lara from Universal Medicine and from the developing parental alienation while at the same time it gave inordinate weight to the disadvantages of change designed to address the deep-seated problems within the family."*[314]

The Court of Appeal considered whether to make an immediate transfer of residence or to remit the matter for a further hearing:

> *"103. It will be apparent from our analysis so far that we find that Lara must be distanced entirely from Universal Medicine. Shared care can therefore only continue if the mother makes an immediate and definitive break with the organisation. Otherwise Lara should move to live with her father. A period with him would give her a sustained opportunity to experience a less anxious and prescriptive way of living. There is a strong argument for saying that the time for such a move has now arrived, that this court should make the necessary orders, and that nothing short of the shock of actually losing Lara's care is likely to impel the mother into doing what is necessary. The alternative is to remit for a further hearing, giving her a final opportunity to dissociate herself in a determined way from Universal Medicine and seek the help she needs to do so. That brings more delay against a deteriorating background, and in the meantime, if the mother does not change her self-defeating stance, matters may get worse.*
>
> *104. We find the arguments finely balanced. In the end, and not without hesitation, we have concluded that the risks involved in postponing a final decision are just worth taking. The current circumstances, adding to the difficulty of an immediate transfer of care, have also been significantly in our minds. With the agreement of the President of the Family Division, we shall remit the father's application for early final determination by him. By determining the matter in this way we are giving the mother a very short respite during which she will have one last chance to take her own steps to leave*

---

[314] ibid., para. 97

Universal Medicine, start intensive therapy, and reverse the process of alienation of Lara from her father. In doing this, we are taking a different course to that taken by the judge, as we now explain. Normally, when remitting a case we would emphasise that this court holds no preconceptions about the outcome. Not so here. In the first place, while the welfare decision will ultimately be for the judge, we remit on the limited basis that the factual foundations for future decisions are contained in the judgment of HHJ Meston QC and of this court, and that the only further evidence that will be needed is in relation to subsequent events. Similarly, the evaluations of the harm being caused to Lara by Universal Medicine and by alienation from her father are left undisturbed by this appeal. Above all, and so that the parties are left in no doubt, we warn that we foresee that without a wholesale transformation in the mother's position the court at the further hearing is likely to find it necessary to transfer Lara's care to her father. The main thing that deters us from making that order now is the possibility, and it is no more than that, that the mother will finally and with a full heart see that she needs to take immediate and unmistakeable steps if she is to continue to play a central part in Lara's upbringing. If that can happen, Lara can return to a balanced arrangement that gives her the best of both parents, something that she is not getting and will not get as matters stand. If it cannot happen, her loss will be very great, but she will gain from growing up in the care of a good parent while attending the same school, and her childhood will not continue to be overshadowed by the baleful influences that have led to the present situation."

In the matter of *Re S (Parental Alienation: Cult: Transfer of Primary Care)*,[315] proceedings were brought back before Williams J. The father's evidence was that contact with the child was poor, she had become more alienated, and continued to exhibit behaviour consistent with Universal Medicine beliefs. Williams J found after hearing evidence (including from the mother, her psychotherapist and the independent social worker) that:

---

[315] [2020] EWHC 1940 (Fam)

"The mother has therefore not come close to achieving the sort of break identified by the Court of Appeal, to showing a wholesale transformation in her position where with a full heart she leaves Universal Medicine, starts intensive therapy and begins the reversal of the process of alienation of the child. Whilst she has taken some steps, they are so limited in their extent and in my assessment so tenuous, that at this stage I am satisfied that, were the child to remain in her care, the process of estrangement would continue and in the short to medium term the child's relationship with the father would be terminated."[316]

Williams J made a transfer of residence order, concluding:

"[…] *I am therefore satisfied that the distress that the child will feel as a result of the separation from her mother and from a period of no contact will be short-term and will not have medium to long-term consequences of a magnitude which in any way approaches the magnitude of the consequences of leaving her in the current position* […]"[317]

Agreed transfers of residence

In *F v M & Ors (Children) (Agreed Transfer of Residence),*[318] a finding of alienation was made against the father. The children had lived with their father after their parents' separation due to the mother being neglectful of their needs while under the influence of alcohol. She had, however, sought professional help and addressed her drinking problem. The father nonetheless continued to regard her as unable to care for the children, and the children had refused contact. There had been no contact for two-years, until a court order in 2020. Thereafter the father had continued to be obstructive. Two months before the hearing the children refused to enter the contact centre where a handover was due to take place, assaulting their mother and locking themselves in the father's car. The father had not intervened during the four-hour incident.

[316] ibid., para. 67

[317] ibid., para. 62

[318] [2021] EWFC 18

The eldest child (X) held particularly negative views of her mother as a result of alienation. Numerous experts' opinions were considered as part of the proceedings including Dr Mark Berelowitz (child and adolescent psychiatrist) and the children's guardian. The guardian was concerned in particular that if X was forced to live with the mother, she would undermine her siblings' placement, and recommended therefore that X remain with the father, and other two children transfer to live with the mother.

The court concluded that there were four options available:

1. All the children to continue to live with the father – the court concluded this was unrealistic as the children's contact with their mother was unlikely to be maintained once the involvement of the children's guardian and the court ended, and there was a high risk the father simply would not be able to promote contact consistently.

2. A shared care arrangement for all three children – this option was supported by the father, however the court concluded it risked causing chaos and upheaval for the children with the numerous handovers each week unlikely to work successfully given the acrimony between the parties.

3. All the children transferring to live with the mother for a period of protective separation of three months from the father.

4. The youngest two children transferring to live with the mother and X remaining with the father.

The court, having ruled out the first two options balanced the remaining two against one another. While option three would enable the children to stay together and repair their relationship with their mother and maternal family, it was contrary to the children's wishes and feelings and the court considered that the children may feel punished which could have the effect of increasing their feelings of negativity towards her. There was also a risk X may run away. Option four on the other hand would mean separation of the children, and it would fail to address X's enmeshed relationship with her father. However, it would give less opportunity for X to undermine her siblings' placement with the mother. Both Dr Berelowitz and the children's guardian reluctantly favoured the fourth option.

In this highly unusual case, it was in fact the father's change in position which tipped the balance: half-way through the hearing he indicated he would support the transfer of all three children to live with the mother for a period of time, though not permanently. This shifted the experts' and the court's assessment in favour of option three:

> "[...] *as Dr Berelowitz has said, F's agreement shifts the balance sufficiently, such that the detriments of this option outweigh the benefits. I agree. Option 3 is not without its risks as already identified, particularly in the short term. However, I must also consider the medium and long-term situation for these children. Dr Berelowitz reiterated that F's attitude is an important factor; the more F supports the plan the more likely a move to a more shared care arrangement in the future will be. However the less supportive F is, the more artificial the plan will be. He thinks F understands this. He said that in summary Y and Z are likely to settle with M. He said he expects they will be sad from time to time but they will settle, but they need to be protected from the undermining that could happen. However, he said one possible outcome which is challenging and sad is that Y and Z settle well, but that X becomes ever dependent on F and evermore isolated. He has considered whether it would be possible to transfer residence for Y and Z, but leave X in F's care. He thinks this would leave X vulnerable.*"[319]

The court concluded that the risks of option four outweighed the risks of option three in terms of the likelihood of harm to the children in the medium to the long-term.

<u>Approaches to implementing a transfer of residence</u>

The dangers of getting the transfer of residence wrong can be severe, and may have significant lasting consequences for the child and the prospect of re-establishing a relationship with the non-resident parent. Before

---

[319] ibid., para. 236

turning to some common approaches the court adopts in managing transfers of residence, it is worth considering some decisions in which the court has reflected upon ineffective and challenging transfers of residence, and what lessons, if any, can be learned from them.

In particular:

- The decision of *Re S (Transfer of Residence)*[320] is the final judgment following a series of widely-reported decisions concerning the subject child, S.[321] In this decision, HHJ Bellamy reflects upon a failed transfer of residence that had involved the initial step of making of an interim care order and placing of the child into foster care. When social workers attempted to facilitate contact between the child and his father in the placement, they were met with persistent refusals. The child would sit with his head in his laps and hands over his ears, and simply refuse to engage with his father. Other behaviours included refusals to take off his coat and shoes, refusals to eat during contact, and repeated comments to his foster carers that he missed his mother and hated his father. Concerns were raised in respect of the child's mental state: he started to experience suicide ideation and was diagnosed with clinical depression as a result of the programme of contact and uncertainty in respect of his long-term living arrangements. The father heeded the recommendation of the children's guardian that the placement in foster care was not working and the child should live with his mother; a decision was taken by the father (who was commended by HHJ Bellamy) to no longer pursue the implementation of the

[320] [2010] EWHC B19 (Fam)

[321] The matter had come before HHJ Bellamy first in in *Re S (Transfer of Residence)* [2010] EWHC 192 (Fam) in which a transfer of residence order was made. The mother appealed, and her appeal was dismissed by the Court of Appeal in *Re S (A Child)* [2010] EWCA Civ 219 (considered in **Chapter 6: The voice of the child**). Thereafter, the transfer of residence was ordered to be effected by the Tipstaff the next day on a hearing which took place on 1 March 2010 in *Re S (A Child)* [2010] EWHC B2 (Fam), which was successfully appealed by the mother in *Re S (A Child)* [2010] EWCA Civ 325.

residence order. The child went to live with the mother with a supervision order made in favour of the local authority.

- The decision in *Re A (Children) (Parental alienation)*[322] is another example of a case in which the court reflected upon a failed transfer of residence (as well as lessons learned from the case more generally, considered in **Chapter 4: Procedurally managing cases involving allegations of parental alienation**). HHJ Wildblood QC reflected that the handover had gone badly wrong, causing significant distress to the children which led to the school becoming concerned and police becoming involved. Within a short period of time after the children began living with their father they ran away several times, refused to eat, and exhibited extreme distress. They returned to their mother less than a month after the hearing and had no further contact with the father thereafter.

- In *Re A and B (Parental Alienation: No. 2)*[323], Keehan J recorded the details of a disastrous transfer of living arrangements that had been made just over three-months prior, considered above in *Re A and B (Parental Alienation: No. 1)*. The day after the transfer took place, the children left their father's home and went to the friend of the mother. It became necessary for the police to secure their return. The children ran away from the father's care a number of times thereafter, going to the home of their former tutor on one occasion (a close friend of the mother, and her former *McKenzie* friend). The friend contacted the local authority thereafter, and a collection order had to be sought out of hours. Before the Tipstaff became involved, the police did, and once against had to use force to secure the children's return back to their father's home. Keehan J suspended the roadmap thereafter of his own motion, and the matter had to be brought back before the court. All was not lost however in this case – the court persisted and the father and his wife was commended for his commitment to re-establishing a relationship with his children. As noted by Keehan J in the fourth

[322] [2019] 9 WLUK 445

[323] [2021] EWHC 2601 (Fam)

judgment *Re A and B (Parental Alienation: No. 4)*[324], the children eventually integrated into their father's care and were noted to be progressing extremely well. A restrictive plan of supervised contact was set up with the mother given her intransigence and failure to accept her responsibility.

If there is one lesson that can be learned from of *Re S (Transfer of Residence)*, considered above, it is that there is often no easy solution in respect of how to effect a transfer of residence. HHJ Bellamy's original decision[325] was that the court should "*grasp the nettle*" in accordance with the expert opinion of Dr Weir (child and adolescent psychiatrist)[326] and effect an enforced transfer by means of the Tipstaff in circumstances where the mother refused to take the child to the father's home herself. HHJ Bellamy concluded that the risks involved in an immediate enforced transfer were outweighed by the potential for longer-term gains, and that further uncertainty or delay was contrary to the child's best interests. However, he was overturned by the Court of Appeal[327] in favour of a stepping-stone foster placement for a period of twenty-one days, only at the end of which the transfer of residence was to be completed. This was felt to be an approach that was "*less confrontational than the immediate*"[328], and an approach that the mother supported and the child was less resistant to. The Court of Appeal's approach ultimately failed, as outlined above. Whether the trial judge's approach would have succeeded does not necessarily follow, but it indicates that implementing a transfer of residence successfully is an imperfect science, subject to varying opinions and with no guarantee of success.

---

324 [2021] EWHC 2603 (Fam)

325 *Re S (A Child)* [2010] EWHC 192 (Fam)

326 Dr Weir suggested: "*The difficulty I have is that although the local authority is hoping reason will prevail and S will come round to accepting the inevitable, I think it is unlikely. The delay allows a period when attitudes can become entrenched, behaving badly, and further risk of harm occurring…at the end after the work and negotiation there will still be the same situation where we have to force him to live with his father. Even if he is willing to go into foster care, which is a good thing because it avoids a scene at the time, the bad thing is that we are not dealing immediately with what is ultimately necessary, that is, to make him to go live with his father.*"

327 *Re S (A Child)* [2010] EWCA Civ 325

328 Ibid., para. 22

Similarly, in *Re A (Children) (Parental alienation)* HHJ Wildblood QC reflected upon the differing opinions from Ms Woodall, Dr Nigel Blagg (a psychologist) and the guardian in respect to the children's alienation, the children's attachment to the father, and crucially the transfer of residence. On the issue of transfer of residence in this case, none of the experts were entirely correct. The court reflected:

> "[…] *i) In written advice to the court two years ago Ms Woodall had said this: 'I have absolutely no doubt, based my extensive experience working with the children should these children be moved to live father, they would emerge from the alienated state of mind within a matter of minutes.' I did not accept view at the hearing when I considered it. Today Ms Woodall acknowledged that she was being over-confident when expressing that opinion.*
>
> *ii) In her evidence at the final hearing Ms Woodall stated that she thought that the children had a 'strong but suppressed attachment' to their father which, when re-awakened, would lead to a successful transfer. Dr Blagg and the Guardian gave evidence to the contrary, saying that the passage of time and the reaction of the children to their father demonstrated that their attachment to him was weak. At the hearing when they gave evidence I accepted the opinions of Dr Blagg and the Guardian. I consider events have shown Dr Blagg and the guardian to be right – the fragility of the children's attachment to their father has been demonstrated very plainly. Ms Woodall retains her opinion and, I have to recognise, this is an issue of differing professional opinions and case dependent.*
>
> *iii) I think that the plans for the transfer of the children to the father involved an underestimation of the likely reaction of the children. Although other experts commented upon those plans, they were devised, principally, by Ms Woodall. I do think that her opinion about the nature of the attachment between the children and the father must have influenced the plans that she devised.* […] *A matter of concern to me, and learning (since I was the judge in charge), was the absence of full and careful discussion with the children's schools notwithstanding that the transfers took place there.*

iv) Following on from the above I think that the extent and depth of the children's alienation from their father and resistance to him were under estimated. That, however, is said with the benefit of hindsight and it could not possibly be right to suggest that the responsibility for that lies with one person. Three experts recommended immediate transfer of residence. Ms Woodall recommended that the transfer should be 'permanent' (meaning long-term) whereas the other two experts supported a short-term transfer with a review – the guardian proposed only a transfer of only two weeks with a review. In any event as matters transpired, I did not follow the advice of Ms Woodall and even so the transfer and period of residence with the father proved to be deeply traumatic."[329]

Part of the difficulty in these sorts of cases is that there remains little published evidence or professional discourse on the best way to manage transfers of residence.[330] In *F v M & Ors (Children) (Agreed Transfer of Residence),* Dr Mark Berelowitz (child and adolescent psychiatrist) provided expert evidence to the court, summarised by the judge as follows:

"He advised that there is no data available from any source on outcomes of change of residence. He could speak anecdotally of the cases with which he has been involved, which he thinks are about 20, and he said that in all of those cases all of the children settled more readily than he feared they might. The one case where it did not work was a case in which he had not been involved from the outset. That was a case of the most extreme alienation that he had come across where the child had no contact with their father for five years. In another case where he knows that the transfer did not work that was due to undermining by the other parent. In that case there were secret telephones and secret meetings at school and a phone was even found under the child's pillow."[331]

---

[329] *Re A (Parental alienation)* [2019] 9 WLUK 445, para. 17

[330] See the comments of Dr Mark Berelowitz, expert child and adolescent psychiatrist in *F v M & Ors. (Children) (Agreed Transfer of Residence)* [2021] EWFC 18 at para. 239

[331] *F v M & Ors. (Children) (Agreed Transfer of Residence)* [2021] EWFC 18, para. 242

When experts are working anecdotally and according to their own individual experience, it becomes difficult to be certain about their recommendations, or to provide any sort of guarantee that any initiative will be met with success. Whilst the need for evidence from an appropriately experienced expert is clear,[332] these cases remain difficult not just because each case is highly dependent upon the facts, but because there are likely to be divergent expert approaches. The court should be particularly cautious of the overly dogmatic expert in this context.

What is of importance however is that professional meetings take place, and a cohesive plan is agreed if possible, or in the event of disagreement, determined and laid out thoroughly by the court. As noted by HHJ Wildblood QC, particular heed should be taken of the difficulties that can be caused by an absence of cohesion and effective collaboration between professionals at the transfer of residence stage:

> *"A particular difficulty in this case has been the absence, at times, of collaborative working by professionals. A particular example of that occurred when an attempt was made to move the children to the father's care. The professionals involved with the court process and the schools had not had sufficient dialogue before that move was attempted and now have very strong and opposing opinions about what occurred and the merits of moving the children from the mother. Pre-planning for the move was inadequate, in my opinion. If professional people show their disagreements, as happened here on the day of transfer, it undermines the process and allows cherry-picking by family members of what they want to hear."*[333]

<u>Guidance for managing a transfer of residence</u>

Whilst it is impossible therefore to adopt a 'one-size-fits-all' approach, it remains useful to consider some of the methods that are commonly employed in previous decisions, and which may, in the appropriate case,

---

332 See the comments of HHJ Bellamy in *Re S (A Child)* [2010] EWHC B19 (Fam) at paras. 59-60

333 *Re A (Children) (Parental alienation)* [2019] 9 WLUK 445, para. 13(vii)

offer ideas as to how to safely implement a transfer of residence when ordered by the court.

Telling the child

The most obvious difficulty and the one which is frequently the starting point for the court's consideration of a transfer of residence is if, when, where and how to tell the child.

In the decision of *F v M & Ors (Children) (Agreed Transfer of Residence),* considered above, Dr Berelowitz suggested (with appropriate caution) that "*the usual practice is to transfer children without notice and from a neutral venue if at all possible*", at school for example.[334] Dr Berelowitz suggests that "*where contact is already taking place, the contact should simply be extended and converted into residence*" and notes that "*telling children in advance that they are going to move increases the likelihood of a traumatic incident.*"[335]

In terms of what the child is told, either before or after attempts to effect a transfer, in this case Dr Berelowitz said "*the children need to be advised in terms that the court has found that F has made it psychologically impossible for them to relax into a rich and full relationship with M*" and that they "*may also need to be told that the consequence of F's approach has been that they will find it very difficult to accept the judgment of the court.*"[336]

The precise wording may be a point of contention between the parties. The wording used in one case may not be appropriate in another. It is frequently sensible for consideration to be given as to whether an agreed

---

[334] An example of this was the decision of Keehan J in *Re H (Parental Alienation)* [2019] EWHC 2723 (Fam). Upon Keehan J announcing his decision to transfer residence at the conclusion of submissions (with judgment reserved), the independent social worker in the case collected the child from school and transported him to his father's home. The paternal family agreed to leave the family home for a short period of time to enable the child to settle into the father's care. Keehan J noted in his judgment that "*this process proceeded without incident and the transition plan to date has been effective*", see para. 39

[335] ibid., para 239

[336] ibid., para. 241

script should be produced. In the event that there is a children's guardian or expert involved, it can be helpful to have their input.

In terms of who is to tell the child, again, there is no easy answer. It may be helpful for the resident parent tell the child, in which case an agreed script is likely to be essential. Whilst this can have the effect of giving the child emotional permission to respond to the move positively, if the resident parent is not on-board there is a risk that such a step risks undermining the transfer and further aligning the child with the alienating parent.

In certain circumstances, the Judge may tell the children about their decision. In *Re A and B (Parental Alienation: No 2)*, Keehan J notes that he himself told the children the outcome of the case and his decision to transfer residence that the Royal Courts of Justice in presence of the expert, Ms Woodall, noting that the children did not take this news well.[337] *Re S (Parental Alienation: Cult: Transfer of Primary Care)*, considered above, Williams J proposed writing a short message to the child for the father to deliver and fall back on in the event difficulties with the child arose after transfer with her acceptance of the situation.[338]

<u>Immediate transfers</u>

The next question will often be: should the transfer of residence be immediately implemented, or alternatively, should a 'stepping-stone' approach be adopted? If the former, consideration must be given as to how to manage such an immediate move to the non-resident parent's address. The latter will involve a transfer to a third location, frequently a foster care placement under the aegis of an interim care order in advance of the final move to the non-resident parent's address (see below).

The ideal in most cases will be that the order is supported by the resident parent, and they assist the transfer. If there is a children's guardian or social worker involved in the case, they may also be able to facilitate the transfer: success is rarely going to be achieved without third-party

---

337 [2021] EWHC 2601 (Fam), para. 3

338 *Re S (Parental Alienation: Cult: Transfer of Primary Care)* [2020] EWHC 1940 (Fam), para. 70

professional involvement and caution will need to be exercised in leaving the handover to the parents, particularly if this has failed before. If the child is to be collected from school and moved to the non-resident parent's address, a decision will need to be made if either of the parents are to be present, or if the collection of the child from school is to be done by a social worker, for example, without either parent present.

'Stepping stone' approaches and the use of interim care orders

An alternative to the immediate transfer can be a 'stepping stone' approach involving a move to a family member, or in certain circumstances into the care of the local authority, prior to the eventual move to the non-resident parent.

The decision of *Re M (Intractable Contact Dispute: Interim Care Order)*[339] (considered further in **Chapter 8: Parental alienation and public children proceedings**) involved an intractable contact dispute in which the mother had persuaded the children that the father had both physically and sexually abused them, and that the paternal grandparents were also physical abusers. The court invited the local authority under section 37 of the 1989 Act to consider taking care proceedings to enable an assessment of the children's relationship with their parents to take place under the aegis of an interim care order. The local authority commenced care proceedings and, as it was impossible to conduct an assessment of the children at home, the court made an interim care order. The children were removed and placed into foster care. Wall J described how "*within a very short space of time, and freed from the need to accommodate the residential parent's false belief system, the children rapidly resumed their relationship with the non-residential parent.*"[340] A residence order (as it was then known) was made in favour of the father.

This case is a useful example of the circumstances in which a 'stepping-stone' approach, involving the making of an interim care order, may be an appropriate step before a transfer of residence decision is effected. The contention in such cases is likely to be the pace of change, and in the

[339] [2003] EWHC 1024 (Fam)

[340] ibid., para. 5

right sort of case an interim holding position can be a stop-gap within which to re-establish contact.

A note of caution: if an interim care order is made at the same time as a transfer of residence order, the factual matrix must be determined. In the case of *Re Z (Interim Care Order) (Rev 1)*[341] it was not, and this ultimately led to a successful appeal. The case involved a local authority's application for care proceedings, including a care plan which provided for the child to be placed in the care of his mother after three to six months of being in a bridging foster placement. The judge approved the interim care order, but stressed that the order was *interim* and that no findings had been made. Thereafter, the child was placed in foster care. The father's appeal against the interim care order was allowed. With regards to the third ground, relevant to the parental alienation point, the judge concluded the following:

> *"The third irregularity concerned the care plan on the basis of which the order was made. As set out above, the plan provided for a short-term bridging placement leading to the placement of Z with his mother in 3 to 6 months, that is to say within the time span of the proceedings. Rehabilitation to his father was expressly ruled out. This plan was approved by the judge but was plainly at variance with the terms of her judgment in which she expressly made it clear that she was not making any findings or reaching a final decision. Further, as the judge had noted in the September judgement, there remain real doubts as to whether Z will ever be reconciled with his mother. Accordingly, the care plan should not have been approved by the judge and the interim care order should not have been made on the basis of that plan."*[342]

In addition, it is important not to forget the warning given by Wall J in *Re M (Intractable Contact Dispute: Interim Care Order)*:

> "*I immediately conscious of course, that the case turns on its particular facts, although the phenomenon it represents is by no means uncommon* [...] *I am also conscious of the fact that there is a tendency in Family Law to see an outcome such as this as a panacea – a one size fits all*

[341] [2020] EWCA Civ 1755

[342] ibid., para. 50

solution. I emphasise that this is not the case, indeed, this judgment comes with a series of strong health warnings."[343]

There is perhaps no better example of the problem with adopting a one size fits all approach to these sorts of proceedings than the judgment of *Re S (Transfer of Residence)*. As outlined above, the decision of HHJ Bellamy records the extent to which the decision to move the child to an interim foster placement and facilitate contact was inappropriate.

Unlike *Re M (Intractable Contact Dispute: Interim Care Order)*, the decision in *Re S (Transfer of Residence)* is not one in which the moved into foster care occurred prior to any final determination of which parent the child should live with. On the contrary, the interim care order was being used as a means of enforcing an order transferring residence from one parent to the other. The failure in this case does not necessarily mean that an interim care order should not be used in the future for such cases, just as *Re M (Intractable Contact Dispute: Interim Care Order)* is not authority for the proposition that an interim care order is appropriate in every case in which a finding of alienation has been made a transfer of residence is being considered. What these decisions indicate is just how contrary results can be when the same approach is employed. Each case is fact specific, and one approach is rarely obviously correct or guaranteed to have the intended effect.

<u>The use of the Tipstaff</u>

Whichever approach is adopted – immediate or 'stepping-stone' – it is only in extreme cases that the court will order that the Tipstaff, the enforcement officer of the court, intervene to transport the child and carry out the transfer. Implementing such an order is likely to have a significant impact on the child in question, and will no doubt be highly contentious.

The legal position in respect of this was considered by HHJ Bellamy in *Re S (Transfer of Residence)*[344], a case in which at first instance HHJ Bellamy had made an order for a transfer of residence from the mother

[343] ibid., paras. 9-10

[344] [2010] EWHC B19 (Fam)

to the father, with the Tipstaff to be engaged to implement the same if necessary:

> "*56. In my judgment of 3 March I made it clear that if the mother did not deliver S to his father's house on 11 March then he should be collected by the Tipstaff the next day and taken by car the two hour journey to his father's home. I noted that S had been informed of the possibility of using the Tipstaff and of Mrs K's* [the children's guardian] *concerns about that approach. In a written statement Mrs K had said*
>
> > *'In the light of the issues raised, I am concerned that S, if forced to live with his father, will sabotage by self harm, either through not eating or trying to run away or jump out of his father's car.'*
>
> *57. In her written submissions Miss Meyer QC, leading counsel for the mother, argued that the forced repatriation of S to his father's home by locking him in a car for two hours represented a breach of S's rights under Art 5. It is important to note that the Court of Appeal*[345] *did not finally dispose of the Art 5 point. Thorpe LJ said this:*
>
> > *'However, I would make three observations on the submission. The first is that it is not necessary for us to rule on the point to dispose of the proceedings before us. The second is that the invocation of the article arises out of circumstances in which the Tipstaff, an officer of the court, was being asked to do no more than a transport job from one home to another. The degree of arrest and detention in that exercise, given the very specialist skills of the Tipstaff and experience of the Tipstaff, is highly questionable. The third point is that, in any event, it seems to me strongly arguable that the Tipstaff's intervention, even if forceful, is covered by the exception contained in paragraph (b) to the article.'*
>
> *58. It was accepted in the Court of Appeal that there is no authority, and in particular no post-Human Rights Act authority, reviewing the power of the judge acting through the Tipstaff. There is still no*

[345] In *Re S (A Child)* [2010] EWCA Civ 325

authority. Art 5.1(b) may cover a situation where the Tipstaff is used to enforce the handing over of a young (i.e. non-Gillick competent) child when the parent with care refuses to comply with an order of the court. Whether the same can be said where the child concerned is a Gillick competent child remains an open question. In this case the question of whether S is Gillick competent was never determined by the Court."

There does not appear to be a subsequent decision involving a transfer of residence decision in the context of a finding of parental alienation which deals with the use of the Tipstaff, presumably given the rarity of such orders in this context. The issues of Gillick competency alongside transfers of residence and the use of Tipstaff are outside the scope of this book, however will warrant careful consideration and may well be the subject of consideration by an appellate court in the future.

Contact between the child and the alienating parent

A further issue that needs to be considered is whether the child is to have any form of contact with the alienating parent, and if so how this is to be managed. Will direct contact be suspended for a period of time to allow a period of uninterrupted adjustment? If so, should indirect contact still continue in some form? Should indirect contact be supervised to ensure that it can be stopped in the event that the alienating parent says or does anything which risks undermining the new placement? If so, who should undertake this supervisory role?

In the case of *Re Y (A Child) (Private Law: Interim Change of Residence)*, considered above, upon the making of an interim transfer of residence the court allowed supervised contact between the child and the mother not less than three times each week for three hours, on the basis that this was supervised. This was in the context of the mother having refused to accept the fact-finding judgment that the father had not sexually abused the child, and her increasing inability to regulate her emotions. Pauffley J noted:

"[...] There is good reason for the requirement of supervision, it seems to me. It is extremely likely that the mother will be very distressed as the result of the impact upon her of recent events. She will find it deeply

upsetting that Y will now be living with her father. It will be vital to monitor the extent to which she is able to present herself in a way that Y will not find disturbing. The Local Authority will make appropriate arrangements as the result of gauging, at every stage, how the mother responds."[346]

In the event that contact is to be suspended, a further issue will be the length of time it should be suspended for, and whether the re-establishment of contact with the alienating parent should be reviewed at a later date. In *Re H (Parental Alienation)*[347] for example, direct contact with the resident parent was suspended for three-months, albeit that indirect contact could take place as advised by the independent social worker instructed in the proceedings.

Indeed, it is common for orders to not set parameters for contact, and for the resumption of contact and subsequent contact with the alienating parent to be determined in consultation with the social worker, children's guardian or an expert, including an independent social worker. In circumstances where the court does not have a crystal ball as to how matters will develop 'on-the-ground' it can make sense for the court to not define contact too rigidly.[348]

As an alternative, the court may deem it in the interests of the child to make an order for contact with the alienating parent that is conditional, and which takes effect in consultation with a third-party professional. This can have the effect of ensuring a later dispute does not arise in respect of the arrangements for contact, however it places the power in the hands of a professional and has a 'carrot-and-stick' effect in that its implementation is dependent upon the parent exhibiting a degree of compliance and change. This was the approach adopted by Keehan J in *Re A and B (Parental Alienation: No. 1)*, considered above, upon making a transfer of residence order. Keehan J had put in place arrangements that provided for no contact during the first month, however provided that

[346] *Re Y (A Child) (Private Law: Interim Change of Residence)* [2014] EWHC 1068 (Fam), para. 26

[347] [2019] EWHC 2723 (Fam)

[348] See for example *Re S (Suspended Residence Order)* [2009] EWHC 1576 (Fam) at para. 132

the mother accepted the judgment *and* the expert (Karen Woodall) considered it in the best interests of the children there was to be indirect contact by way of a telephone call in the days after the judgment and over the Christmas break. After this month, direct contact was then to take place preferably on a supervised basis, once every three weeks for a period of four hours, progressing after three months to staying contact once every three weeks from a Friday evening to Sunday evening, as well as during the holidays. Ultimately, the transfer failed in the first instance, but eventually took place whereupon the children integrated well into the care of the father and his wife. Due to this the matter had to come back before the court, including to consider contact going forwards with the mother. In the fourth decision *Re A and B (Parental Alienation: No. 4)*, Keehan J endorsed a roadmap for contact that had been prepared by Karen Woodall that provided for restrictive supervised direct and indirect contact with the mother. The court deemed that the mother's lack of engagement and acceptance of her past role merited a more restrictive plan of contact.[349]

Similarly, in *Re S (Parental Alienation: Cult: Transfer of Primary Care),* considered above, there was to be no direct or indirect contact over the extended summer vacation to enable the child to settle. Thereafter, it was said that some supervised time, with the assistance of the independent social worker, could be introduced, designed to minimise any distress and ensure the child was still protected from the mother's dangerous views on Universal Medicine. The progression to unsupervised contact was to be decided in consultation between the independent social worker and the father, considering whether the child had made the *"emotional leap to acceptance that her home is to be with the father for the future."*[350]

A frequent cause of disruption to a new placement, post transfer, may indeed be unsupervised indirect contact either through mobile phone or other devices. Such contact can represent for the child a constant link to the alienating parent, and, in the event that that parent does not support the move, may give rise to a sustained undermining of the new

---

349 *Re A and B (Parental Alienation: No. 4)* [2021] EWHC 2603 (Fam), para. 19

350 *Re S (Parental Alienation: Cult: Transfer of Primary Care)* [2020] EWHC 190 (Fam), para. 69

placement. A decision will have to be made about how this is to be managed, in particular with older children where it may be somewhat draconian to completely remove their mobile phone in the immediate aftermath of the transfer.

CHAPTER EIGHT

PARENTAL ALIENATION AND PUBLIC CHILDREN PROCEEDINGS

This Chapter will consider the intersection between private and public children proceedings. In particular, consideration will be given to circumstances in which parental alienation has become severe enough for the public law threshold to be deemed to have been crossed, and to warrant care proceedings being issued.

<u>Threshold</u>

Under section 31(2) of the 1989 Act, the court can consider making a public law order – namely a care order (placing the child in the care of the designated local authority) or supervision order – if it is satisfied that:

a. The child concerned is suffering, or is likely to suffer, significant harm; and

b. The harm, or likelihood of harm is attributable to –

    i. The care given to the child, or likely to be given to him if the order was not made, not being what it would be reasonable to expect a parent to give him; or

    ii. The child's being beyond parental control.

'Harm' is defined as ill treatment or the impairment of health (including physical or mental health) or development. This includes, for example, impairment suffered from seeing or hearing the ill-treatment of another. Crucially, ill-treatment includes forms of ill-treatment which are not physical (section 31(9)).

In considering whether harm is significant to a child's health or development, the child's health and development must be compared with that which could reasonably be expected of a similar child (section 31(10)).

The court may make an interim care order or interim supervision order with respect of the child concerned if satisfied that there are reasonable grounds for believing that the circumstances with respect to the child are as mentioned in section 31(2) of the 1989 Act (section 38).

For the purposes of this book, it suffices to say that it is possible for cases of high parental conflict, including circumstances involving active alienation of a child by one parent, to meet the threshold of significant harm.

Local authority assessments

In the event that there is local authority involvement with a family, it may be the case that assessments have already been undertaken or are underway to determine the individual needs of the subject child, what services to provide and what further action the local authority should undertake.

At the most extreme end of the spectrum, where a local authority has reasonable cause for suspecting that a child who lives, or is found, in their area is suffering, or is likely to suffer significant harm, pursuant to section 47(1), it should make, or cause to be made, such enquiries as it considers necessary to enable it to decide whether it should take any action to safeguard or promote the child's welfare. These enquiries, in particular, should be directed towards establishing whether the local authority should make any application under the 1989 Act, including for care orders or supervision orders (section 47(3)(a)(i)).

Frequently, public children disputes are much more concerned with immediate and obvious concerns regarding parenting. Whilst parental conflict may be a factor in establishing threshold, it may not be pleaded as 'parental alienation.' This may be because there is an insufficient evidence base, in particular in situations where it has not been identified previously. This is likely to be because the local authority is more concerned with outlining threshold based on definitive events.

In cases where there is an established factual matrix from previous proceedings, it may be obvious that the child is suffering or likely to suffer significant harm as a result of parental alienation. On this basis, proceedings may commence as public law proceedings from the outset.

It is more likely, however, that cases involving allegations of alienation start out as private children disputes, and the local authority's intervention follows at a later date. Frequently, this will occur after the factual matrix has been determined, and it has been found that the child has been subjected to alienating behaviours that are having a harmful impact upon their welfare, which the court determines may meet the threshold for public law intervention.

Section 37 reports

In circumstances where the court determines that public law intervention may be necessary, and a care or supervision order may be appropriate, the court is able to invite the local authority to undertake an investigation pursuant to section 37 of the 1989 Act. This says as follows:

> *(1) Where, in any family proceedings in which a question arises with respect to the welfare of any child, it appears to the court that it may be appropriate for a care or supervision order to be made with respect to him, the court may direct the appropriate authority to undertake an investigation of the child's circumstances.*
>
> *(2) Where the court gives a direction under this section the local authority concerned shall, when undertaking the investigation, consider whether they should—*
>
> > *(a) apply for a care order or for a supervision order with respect to the child;*
> >
> > *(b) provide services or assistance for the child or his family; or*
> >
> > *(c) take any other action with respect to the child.*

(3) Where a local authority undertake an investigation under this section, and decide not to apply for a care order or supervision order with respect to the child concerned, they shall inform the court of—

(a) their reasons for so deciding;

(b) any service or assistance which they have provided, or intend to provide, for the child and his family; and

(c) any other action which they have taken, or propose to take, with respect to the child.

(4) The information shall be given to the court before the end of the period of eight weeks beginning with the date of the direction, unless the court otherwise directs.

(5) The local authority named in a direction under subsection (1) must be—

(a) the authority in whose area the child is ordinarily resident; or

(b) where the child is not ordinarily resident in the area of a local authority, the authority within whose area any circumstances arose in consequence of which the direction is being given.

(6) If, on the conclusion of any investigation or review under this section, the authority decide not to apply for a care order or supervision order with respect to the child—

(a) they shall consider whether it would be appropriate to review the case at a later date; and

(b) if they decide that it would be, they shall determine the date on which that review is to begin.

It is important to emphasise that the purpose of a section 37 report is not to determine the veracity of the parents' competing allegations; the local authority's investigation is solely directed at determining its course of action going forwards.

Wall J (as he then was) in the case of *Re M (Intractable Contact Dispute: Interim Care Order)*[351] (considered in **Chapter 7: Transfers of residence**) has provided robust guidance on the use of section 37 in high conflict contact cases. In the circumstances of this case, the local authority had completed its section 37 enquiries and issued care proceedings. The section 37 investigation in this instance had been ordered following protracted private law proceedings in which multiple orders had been breached, and the mother had been found to have emotionally manipulated the child and repeatedly made false allegations against the father and paternal grandparents of physical and sexual abuse.

The court outlined the following guidance as being essential when consideration is being given to directing a section 37 report:

> *"8. First, of course, s 37, which I set out at para [121] of this judgment, can only be used if the facts of the case meet its criteria. It must appear to the court that 'it may be appropriate for a care or supervision order to be made' with respect to the children in question. In other words, at the very lowest, the court must be satisfied that there are reasonable grounds for believing that the circumstances with respect to the children meet the threshold criteria under s 31(2) – that is to say that the children are suffering or are likely to suffer significant harm. Section 37 is, accordingly, a well-focused tool, to be used only when the case fits its criteria.*
>
> *9. It is sometimes forgotten that the court has the power to make an interim care order when it gives a direction under s 37 (see s 38(1)(b) of the Children Act 1989). The definition of 'specified proceedings' (ibid s 41(6)(b)) includes private law proceedings for contact or residence orders in which the court has given a direction under s 37(1) and has made or is considering whether to make an interim care order. In these circumstances a children's guardian must be appointed under s 41(1) unless the court is satisfied that it is not necessary to do so in order to safeguard the children's interests.*
>
> *10. In the instant case, the children were already represented by CAFCASS Legal when I made the s 37 direction. Had they not been,*

[351] [2003] EWHC 1024 (Fam)

I am in no doubt that I would have appointed a guardian to represent them.

11. Although this case is but an example, it does seem to me that it is possible to extract some general considerations of wider application from it. I put these forward tentatively, as each case is different, and what fits one may not fit another. Some points are self-evident, but need stating nonetheless. I will state them in short form and then expand on them where necessary:

> *(1) The court must be satisfied that the criteria for ordering a s 37 report are satisfied (see para [8] above).*
>
> *(2) The action contemplated (removal of the children from the residential parent's care either for an assessment or with a view to a change of residence) must be in the children's best interests. The consequences of the removal must be thought through. There must, in short, be a coherent care plan of which temporary or permanent removal from the residential parent's care is an integral part.*
>
> *(3) Where, as here, the allegation is that the children have been sexually or physically abused by the absent parent, the court must have held a hearing in which those issues were addressed, and findings made about them (see para [12] below).*
>
> *(4) The court must spell out its reasons for making the s 37 order very carefully, and a transcript (or a very full note) of the judgment should be made available to the local authority at the earliest opportunity (see paras [13]–[14] below).*
>
> *(5) The children should be separately represented (see paras [15]–[16] below).*
>
> *(6) Preferably, the s 37 report should be supported by professional or expert advice (see para [17] below).*

(7) Judicial continuity is essential. Apart from saving time and resources, this means that applications can be made to the judge at short notice, and she or he can keep tight control over it.

(8) Undue delay must be avoided (see paras [18] and [19] below).

(9) The case may need to be kept under review if (as in the instant case) the decision of the court is to move the children from one parent to another (see paras [20] and [21] below).

Findings of fact

12. In the instant case, the residential parent asserted that the children had been sexually and physically abused by the non-residential and the latter's parents. This was not true. I was, however, only able to proceed on the basis that it was not true because there had been clear and compelling findings by an experienced circuit judge, and I was able to confirm those findings by the evidence I heard. It is, in my judgment, very important that the local authority should know the court's findings and prepare its report on the basis of those findings. In an intractable contact dispute, where the residential parent is putting forward an allegedly factual basis for contact not taking place, there is no substitute, in my judgment, for findings by the court as to whether or not there is any substance to the allegations.

Letting the local authority know the reasons for making the order

13. In my judgment, it is vital for the local authority to know the judge's thinking in making the order. Even if such an order is made urgently, a note of the reasons for it should, in my judgment, be prepared and made available to the local authority. Apart from anything else, clear reasons for the order save a great deal of time, and enable the local authority to focus on the salient points. In the instant case, I reserved judgment and shortly afterwards handed down the first of the two judgments set out below in a form designed to be read by both the parties and the local authority. In its original form, the first judgment was cross-referenced to the court bundles which were also disclosed to the local authority. Such a course may not be practical in other cases, particularly where the report is urgently required. However, it is not enough, in my judgment, for the local authority simply to be told the judge has ordered a s 37 report. The local authority needs to know why the judge has done so.

14. It is prosaic thought, but when making a s 37 order the court should be clear about how the order is going to be communicated to the local authority and by whom. There is nothing more likely to cause delay than the absence of a speedy mechanism for conveying the order to the local authority. I have on at least one occasion written short reasons, told the bar what they were, and then sent them by facsimile to an identified officer of the local authority.

Separate representation

15. It is my view that one of the prime categories for the tandem model of separate representation in private law proceedings is where all contact has ceased and the issue of contact has become intractable. Children in this situation frequently have an interest in the proceedings and in the outcome which is independent from the viewpoint being advanced by each of their parents.

16. As I have stated in para [10], in the instant case the children were already represented by the time the case reached me. Generally, however, if an intractable contact dispute has reached the stage where it is ripe for a s 37 report, then in my judgment it is at a stage where separate representation is necessary. If the report recommends care proceedings, the guardian already in place can act as guardian in those proceedings. If it does not, the court is going to have to try an alternative approach. This is an area where the independent tandem model, in my experience, has proved extremely helpful in providing advice and, where necessary, obtaining expert evidence.

Expert advice

17. In the instant case, as the first judgment shows, a complication was that removal was supported by the children's guardian and opposed by the psychiatrist she had instructed to advise on the children's behalf. It is, however, of material assistance to a court if there has been an investigation by an expert who has come to the view that the children are suffering significant harm and that local authority intervention is necessary. This advice does not, however, in my judgment necessarily have to come from a psychiatrist or psychologist. A competent Children and Family Court Advisory and Support Service (CAFCASS) report by a court reporter should identify the problem.

Delay

18. Where a report is ordered, the date for its receipt and for the giving of further directions must be specified. If a guardian is required, and CAFCASS Legal cannot allocate a guardian immediately, a guardian from another source should be appointed. This can either be a specialist solicitor who can then instruct an independent social worker to undertake the guardian role, or an organisation such as the National Youth Advocacy Service (NYAS).

19. In this case, there was inexcusable delay between 8 February 2001 when the order inviting the Official Solicitor to represent the children was made, and 27 September 2001, when the children were joined as parties to the proceedings. The very fact of ordering a s 37 report involves an element of delay. It is very important that this should be minimised. This requires strict judicial control: hence one of the needs for judicial continuity.

Keeping the case under review

20. The object of care proceedings following the s 37 report in this case was to relieve the children from the significant harm they were suffering with their residential parent, and to restore their relationship with their non-residential parent. In the longer term, the aim was to enable the children to retain a good relationship with both parents. That objective is defeated if, having regained their relationship with the non-residential parent they then lose it with the parent from whose care they have been removed.

21. In my judgment, therefore, it may well be desirable for the case to be kept under review – alternatively, as here, the court should satisfy

> *itself that mechanisms were in place to address the issue of ongoing contact.*
>
> *Generally*
>
> *22. It has to be acknowledged that the s 37 process is heavy on resources and takes time. At the same time, the stakes for the children are very high. Decisions to remove children from the homes they know and in which they feel secure are difficult. The consequences can be traumatic.*
>
> *23. As it happened, the residential parent in the instant case was the mother, and the non-residential parent was the father. I wish to make it as clear as I can, however, that this judgment is neither pro-father nor anti-mother. As with every case tried in the Family Division and by circuit and district judges and magistrates up and down the country day in and day out, it is my attempt to apply the welfare principle in s 1 of the Children Act 1989 to the facts of the particular case."*

The usual process in circumstances where the local authority decides to make an application for a public law order as a result of a section 37 investigation is for the private law proceedings to be stayed, or alternatively consolidated with the new public law proceedings.

Interim care and supervision orders

Whether in the context of public law proceedings, or private proceedings which have taken a public course as a result of a section 37 investigation or otherwise, in any case where the court decides to make an interim care or interim supervision order, the court must be satisfied that there are reasonable grounds to believe the children is suffering, or at risk of suffering, significant harm.[352]

The making of an interim care order does not necessarily indicate that the child will be removed from the resident parent. Whilst in certain cases the alienation is so severe that it is deemed necessary to remove a child

[352] Children Act 1989, section 38(2)

and place them in foster care to prevent further emotional harm,[353] this will not always be appropriate, and each case turns on its own facts. As with transfers of residence, the benefits of preventing further emotional harm and potentially salvaging a relationship with the non-resident parent need to be carefully balanced against the risks that a move may involve, including the compound the negative perceptions of the subject child. It may be appropriate to remove the child from the current home environment under an interim care order and place with family members as a less draconian alternative. It may be equally appropriate to manage the situation by keeping the child with the alienating parent, but keeping matters under review through an interim supervision order.

In circumstances in which there is a move to local authority foster care the advantages of this largely stem from the child being removed from the influence of the alienating parent and into a neutral environment, something which may better advance the project of re-establishing contact. *Re S and T (care proceedings following private law dispute)*[354] was a recent case in which it was found that the mother has made false allegations of domestic abuse and sexual abuse against the father in an attempt to prevent him having a relationship with his daughters. The children had been moved into local authority foster care under an interim care order during public law proceedings which had been commenced following a section 37 report. While in local authority foster care the children recommenced indirect contact with their father and thereafter direct contact. Matters progressed to such an extent that overnight stays were introduced and were reportedly going well, with both children telling their foster carer they wished to spend longer periods of time with their father during the weekends. At the conclusion of the care proceedings, the local authority's position was that the children should move to full-time care of their father, and continue to have regular supervised time with their mother. The local authority's care plan was approved by the judge, and a child arrangements order was made for the children to live with their father and his partner.

---

353 See for example *Re S and T (care proceedings following private law dispute)* [2021] EWFC B54

354 [2021] EWFC B54

The case of *Re M (Intractable Contact Dispute: Interim Care Order)* was an unusual situation in which it was deemed appropriate to make an interim care order alongside an order that the child would live with the father. However, the child arrangements order was only to take effect at a date to be agreed between the father and the local authority, whereupon the interim care order would be discharged, and it was determined that a supervision order would be in place for two-years thereafter.

The use of interim care orders as a means of facilitating transfers of residence is discussed in detail in **Chapter 7: Transfers of residence**.

Final care orders

It may further be appropriate to make a final care order, including an order for the child to remain in long-term foster care, in circumstances where the child has been alienated. This was the case in *Re A (Parental Alienation by the Non-Resident Parent)* [2022].[355] The local authority's care plan was for the children to remain in long-term foster care, with the plan being to rehabilitate them to the care of their mother when the time was right. This plan was supported by the mother and the guardian, and endorsed by HHJ McKinnell. The children had expressed worrying behaviour towards their mother, including saying they hate her, fantasising about attacking her with a knife, threatening her, being angry and aggressive towards her, and calling her a host of names. All the experts in the case were clear they had been influenced by the father, aligned themselves with him and mirrored his viewed and feelings, and had been alienated from the mother. The Judge agreed. As part of the local authority's care plan, prior to any reunification with the mother, was a robust therapeutic plan to rectify the damage caused to the children by their father.

Involvement of the local authority in private law disputes

It has recently been acknowledged by Knowles J in the case of *Re S*[356] that there remains much work to be done by many local authorities in grappling with the interplay between private and public children

355 [2022] 1 WLUK 397

356 [2020] EWHC 217 (Fam)

disputes, and in particular, the role that the local authority plays in cases of complex private children disputes.

Re S involved a local authority issuing public law proceedings within pre-existing private law proceedings, on the basis that the children had suffered and were likely to suffer significant emotional harm arising from the mother's unfounded allegations that the fathers of the children had physically and sexually abused the children during contact. The court made unambiguous findings (on the basis of the mother's acceptance that she no longer pursued the same) that the children had not been physically or sexually abused, although it was questioned whether the mother's behaviour could be described as parental alienation when the child attended and engaged well with contact when possible.

Knowles J went on to make the following important comments:

> *"63. It is my perception that local authorities may be ill-equipped to grapple with complex private law proceedings where there are allegations of abuse made by one parent against the other. Though it is trite to observe that social workers are well aware that children can be harmed in such situations, translating that knowledge into effective social work practice is rather more difficult. There is little specific assistance to be derived from the contents of "Working Together To Safeguard Children". Furthermore, an organisational resistance to sustained involvement in what is seen as essentially a dispute between separated parents may also be in play in circumstances where local authorities are hard pressed to manage their child protection workload. This case demonstrates the need to develop more coherent and child focused ways of working with families such as this one.*
>
> [...]
>
> *69. What strikes me as beyond argument was the unhelpful nature of the piecemeal assessments conducted by the local authority in this case. Assessments were brief and conducted in response to allegations made by the mother. This case cried out for a comprehensive assessment of the family which might have led to a more informed understanding of both the mother's anxieties around X's contact with her father and her failure to promote Y's contact with his father once that broke down in*

November 2017. It may also have identified at a much earlier date the need for either a psychological or a mental health assessment of the mother.

70. However, and for the avoidance of doubt, my criticisms of the social work practice in this case does not mean that professionals were to blame for the repeated allegations made by the mother which disrupted the children's relationship with their respective fathers. It was the mother's erroneous beliefs which drove the making of allegations and not the responses of professionals. This mother was in search of evidence to prove that which she wrongly believed to be true and, no matter who she spoke to, the allegations aimed at AB kept coming. Even repeated attendances at court between October 2017 and May 2019 failed to modify the mother's behaviour. The videos made of X were a truly desperate and profoundly damaging step taken by the mother in pursuit of what she believed AB to be doing to their child.

71. In summary, what might be gleaned from this case of benefit to professionals working with complex private law disputes? The following matters suggest themselves:

a) repeated section 47 investigations, which are not anchored to a comprehensive family assessment, are ultimately of little benefit;

b) greater respect needs to be given to the views of professionals who see the family more often than most social workers ever do;

c) in the interests of effective multi-disciplinary working, social workers may, on occasion, have good reason to challenge the views of other professionals. Ensuring other professionals understand the local authority's concerns and are updated as to recent events may assist that process;

d) families should be referred to sources of guidance and support or offered it as part of the local authority's intervention. This should happen sooner rather than later. The mother might well have benefitted from guidance about separated parenting and child development. Both parents would also have benefitted from

> *advice and guidance in managing contact handovers and in communicating with each other about their child;*
>
> *e) mediation services (aimed at separated parents and with appropriate expertise in dealing with complex contact cases) might have helped this family at an early stage of the proceedings;*
>
> *f) delay in commissioning expert assessments is damaging. This case would have benefitted from an early specialist assessment which might have obviated the need for these proceedings;*
>
> *g) such cases require a high degree of professional skill from social workers and their managers and, in my view, should not be allocated to trainee or inexperienced social workers. These can be some of the most frustrating and difficult cases to work because of the high levels of entrenched parental conflict into which children are inevitably drawn. Better training about the complex issues these cases demonstrate, such as repeated but unsubstantiated allegations of abuse, seems to me to be urgently needed both for local authority social workers and their managers.*
>
> *I recognise that implementing these suggestions, if they are to be useful, will need not just commitment from senior managers in local authorities but also substantial investment in services and training. Provision of the necessary resources will be for others to address but this case demonstrates they are urgently needed."*

The suggestions made in this judgment provide helpful guidance for cases at the cross-section of private and public children proceedings. Knowles J raises issues that often exacerbate and delay proceedings, but ultimately comes to the conclusion that additional resources need to be allocated to address such issues.

Conclusions

There can be significant progress made in unlocking a case involving parental alienation through the case being before the court as a result of a public law application. There are benefits that may arise from continued social work involvement with the family, including the quick identification and reporting of contact being obstructed, and the ability for the court to have a more constant and attentive eye on what is happening 'on the ground.' The threat or realisation of public law proceedings can be a powerful incentive for the alienating parent to change their approach, and begin to co-operate with the court's orders in cases where there are multiple breaches of interim child arrangements orders.

In circumstances where the parties do not have the means to fund expert assessments, the costs of the same may be met by the public purse (in the event that public law proceedings are issued the parties are entitled to non-means and non-merit tested public funding). Further, in certain (though limited) circumstances, the local authority may be prevailed upon to assist with funding therapeutic work that is deemed necessary for the children. However, experience suggests that local authorities are likely to guard their funds closely, and it must be acknowledged that funding challenges are still likely to arise in some shape or form as a result of burdens on the public purse.

Whilst in appropriate cases public law proceedings can be helpful in safeguarding the child from further harm as a result of alienation and progressing the relationship between the non-resident parent and child, these sorts of proceedings are relatively uncommon and the instigation of public law proceedings should not be viewed as a panacea in all cases. The case of *Re A (Children) (Parental alienation),*[357] which has been discussed at length within this text, is a powerful reminder of that. In that instance, even in the context of public law proceedings and significant social worker intervention, the transfer of residence that was ordered failed to effect change in the outlook of the children, and the local authority withdrew public law proceedings on the basis that the transfer of residence had been deeply traumatic for the child, and the placement had broken down.

---

[357] [2019] 9 WLUK 445

MORE BOOKS BY LAW BRIEF PUBLISHING

A selection of our other titles available now:-

'A Practical Guide to Document Signing and Electronic Signatures for Conveyancers' by Lorraine Richardson
'A Practical Guide to Transgender Law' by Robin Moira White & Nicola Newbegin
'Artificial Intelligence – The Practical Legal Issues (2nd Edition)' by John Buyers
'A Practical Guide to Residential Freehold Conveyancing' by Lorraine Richardson
'A Practical Guide to Pensions on Divorce for Lawyers' by Bryan Scant
'A Practical Guide to Challenging Sham Marriage Allegations in Immigration Law' by Priya Solanki
'A Practical Guide to Legal Rights in Scotland' by Sarah-Jane Macdonald
'A Practical Guide to New Build Conveyancing' by Paul Sams & Rebecca East
'A Practical Guide to Defending Barristers in Disciplinary Cases' by Marc Beaumont
'A Practical Guide to Inherited Wealth on Divorce' by Hayley Trim
'A Practical Guide to Practice Direction 12J and Domestic Abuse in Private Law Children Proceedings' by Rebecca Cross & Malvika Jaganmohan
'A Practical Guide to Confiscation and Restraint' by Narita Bahra QC, John Carl Townsend, David Winch
'A Practical Guide to the Law of Forests in Scotland' by Philip Buchan
'A Practical Guide to Health and Medical Cases in Immigration Law' by Rebecca Chapman & Miranda Butler
'A Practical Guide to Bad Character Evidence for Criminal Practitioners by Aparna Rao
'A Practical Guide to Extradition Law post-Brexit' by Myles Grandison et al
'A Practical Guide to Hoarding and Mental Health for Housing Lawyers' by Rachel Coyle
'A Practical Guide to Psychiatric Claims in Personal Injury – 2nd Edition' by Liam Ryan
'Stephens on Contractual Indemnities' by Richard Stephens

'A Practical Guide to the EU Succession Regulation' by Richard Frimston
'A Practical Guide to Solicitor and Client Costs – 2nd Edition' by Robin Dunne
'Constructive Dismissal – Practice Pointers and Principles' by Benjimin Burgher
'A Practical Guide to Religion and Belief Discrimination Claims in the Workplace' by Kashif Ali
'A Practical Guide to the Law of Medical Treatment Decisions' by Ben Troke
'Fundamental Dishonesty and QOCS in Personal Injury Proceedings: Law and Practice' by Jake Rowley
'A Practical Guide to the Law in Relation to School Exclusions' by Charlotte Hadfield & Alice de Coverley
'A Practical Guide to Divorce for the Silver Separators' by Karin Walker
'The Right to be Forgotten – The Law and Practical Issues' by Melissa Stock
'A Practical Guide to Planning Law and Rights of Way in National Parks, the Broads and AONBs' by James Maurici QC, James Neill et al
'A Practical Guide to Election Law' by Tom Tabori
'A Practical Guide to the Law in Relation to Surrogacy' by Andrew Powell
'A Practical Guide to Claims Arising from Fatal Accidents – 2nd Edition' by James Patience
'A Practical Guide to the Ownership of Employee Inventions – From Entitlement to Compensation' by James Tumbridge & Ashley Roughton
'A Practical Guide to Asbestos Claims' by Jonathan Owen & Gareth McAloon
'A Practical Guide to Stamp Duty Land Tax in England and Northern Ireland' by Suzanne O'Hara
'A Practical Guide to the Law of Farming Partnerships' by Philip Whitcomb
'Covid-19, Homeworking and the Law – The Essential Guide to Employment and GDPR Issues' by Forbes Solicitors
'Covid-19 and Criminal Law – The Essential Guide' by Ramya Nagesh
'Covid-19 and Family Law in England and Wales – The Essential Guide' by Safda Mahmood
'A Practical Guide to the Law of Unlawful Eviction and Harassment – 2nd Edition' by Stephanie Lovegrove
'Covid-19, Brexit and the Law of Commercial Leases – The Essential Guide' by Mark Shelton
'A Practical Guide to Costs in Personal Injury Claims – 2nd Edition' by Matthew Hoe

'A Practical Guide to the General Data Protection Regulation (GDPR) – 2nd Edition' by Keith Markham
'Ellis on Credit Hire – Sixth Edition' by Aidan Ellis & Tim Kevan
'A Practical Guide to Working with Litigants in Person and McKenzie Friends in Family Cases' by Stuart Barlow
'Protecting Unregistered Brands: A Practical Guide to the Law of Passing Off' by Lorna Brazell
'A Practical Guide to Secondary Liability and Joint Enterprise Post-Jogee' by Joanne Cecil & James Mehigan
'A Practical Guide to the Pre-Action RTA Claims Protocol for Personal Injury Lawyers' by Antonia Ford
'A Practical Guide to Neighbour Disputes and the Law' by Alexander Walsh
'A Practical Guide to Forfeiture of Leases' by Mark Shelton
'A Practical Guide to Coercive Control for Legal Practitioners and Victims' by Rachel Horman
'A Practical Guide to Rights Over Airspace and Subsoil' by Daniel Gatty
'Tackling Disclosure in the Criminal Courts – A Practitioner's Guide' by Narita Bahra QC & Don Ramble
'A Practical Guide to the Law of Driverless Cars – Second Edition' by Alex Glassbrook, Emma Northey & Scarlett Milligan
'A Practical Guide to TOLATA Claims' by Greg Williams
'A Practical Guide to Elderly Law – 2nd Edition' by Justin Patten
'A Practical Guide to Responding to Housing Disrepair and Unfitness Claims' by Iain Wightwick
'A Practical Guide to the Construction and Rectification of Wills and Trust Instruments' by Edward Hewitt
'A Practical Guide to the Law of Bullying and Harassment in the Workplace' by Philip Hyland
'How to Be a Freelance Solicitor: A Practical Guide to the SRA-Regulated Freelance Solicitor Model' by Paul Bennett
'A Practical Guide to Prison Injury Claims' by Malcolm Johnson
'A Practical Guide to the Small Claims Track - 2nd Edition' by Dominic Bright
'A Practical Guide to Advising Clients at the Police Station' by Colin Stephen McKeown-Beaumont
'A Practical Guide to Antisocial Behaviour Injunctions' by Iain Wightwick

'Practical Mediation: A Guide for Mediators, Advocates, Advisers, Lawyers, and Students in Civil, Commercial, Business, Property, Workplace, and Employment Cases' by Jonathan Dingle with John Sephton
'The Mini-Pupillage Workbook' by David Boyle
'A Practical Guide to Crofting Law' by Brian Inkster
'A Practical Guide to Spousal Maintenance' by Liz Cowell
'A Practical Guide to the Law of Domain Names and Cybersquatting' by Andrew Clemson
'A Practical Guide to the Law of Gender Pay Gap Reporting' by Harini Iyengar
'A Practical Guide to the Rights of Grandparents in Children Proceedings' by Stuart Barlow
'NHS Whistleblowing and the Law' by Joseph England
'Employment Law and the Gig Economy' by Nigel Mackay & Annie Powell
'A Practical Guide to Noise Induced Hearing Loss (NIHL) Claims' by Andrew Mckie, Ian Skeate, Gareth McAloon
'An Introduction to Beauty Negligence Claims – A Practical Guide for the Personal Injury Practitioner' by Greg Almond
'Intercompany Agreements for Transfer Pricing Compliance' by Paul Sutton
'Zen and the Art of Mediation' by Martin Plowman
'A Practical Guide to the SRA Principles, Individual and Law Firm Codes of Conduct 2019 – What Every Law Firm Needs to Know' by Paul Bennett
'A Practical Guide to Adoption for Family Lawyers' by Graham Pegg
'A Practical Guide to Industrial Disease Claims' by Andrew Mckie & Ian Skeate
'A Practical Guide to Redundancy' by Philip Hyland
'A Practical Guide to Vicarious Liability' by Mariel Irvine
'A Practical Guide to Applications for Landlord's Consent and Variation of Leases' by Mark Shelton
'A Practical Guide to Relief from Sanctions Post-Mitchell and Denton' by Peter Causton
'A Practical Guide to Equity Release for Advisors' by Paul Sams
'A Practical Guide to Financial Services Claims' by Chris Hegarty
'The Law of Houses in Multiple Occupation: A Practical Guide to HMO Proceedings' by Julian Hunt
'Occupiers, Highways and Defective Premises Claims: A Practical Guide Post-Jackson – 2nd Edition' by Andrew Mckie

'A Practical Guide to Financial Ombudsman Service Claims' by Adam Temple & Robert Scrivenor
'A Practical Guide to Advising Schools on Employment Law' by Jonathan Holden
'A Practical Guide to Running Housing Disrepair and Cavity Wall Claims: 2nd Edition' by Andrew Mckie & Ian Skeate
'A Practical Guide to Holiday Sickness Claims – 2nd Edition' by Andrew Mckie & Ian Skeate
'Arguments and Tactics for Personal Injury and Clinical Negligence Claims' by Dorian Williams
'A Practical Guide to Drone Law' by Rufus Ballaster, Andrew Firman, Eleanor Clot
'A Practical Guide to Compliance for Personal Injury Firms Working With Claims Management Companies' by Paul Bennett
'RTA Allegations of Fraud in a Post-Jackson Era: The Handbook – 2nd Edition' by Andrew Mckie
'RTA Personal Injury Claims: A Practical Guide Post-Jackson' by Andrew Mckie
'On Experts: CPR35 for Lawyers and Experts' by David Boyle
'An Introduction to Personal Injury Law' by David Boyle

These books and more are available to order online direct from the publisher at www.lawbriefpublishing.com, where you can also read free sample chapters. For any queries, contact us on 0844 587 2383 or mail@lawbriefpublishing.com.

Our books are also usually in stock at www.amazon.co.uk with free next day delivery for Prime members, and at good legal bookshops such as Wildy & Sons.

We are regularly launching new books in our series of practical day-to-day practitioners' guides. Visit our website and join our free newsletter to be kept informed and to receive special offers, free chapters, etc.

You can also follow us on Twitter at www.twitter.com/lawbriefpub.

www.ingramcontent.com/pod-product-compliance
Lightning Source LLC
LaVergne TN
LVHW050302210926
848481LV00014BA/592

* 9 7 8 1 9 1 3 7 1 5 1 8 2 *